Food
for
Thought

A combination of life, karate,
cooking and disability
by David Croft

Matador
5 Weir Road
Kibworth Beauchamp_
Leicester LE8 0LQ, UK
Tel:_(+44) 116 279 2299
Fax: (+44) 116 279 2277
Email: books@troubador.co.uk
Web:_www.troubador.co.uk/matador

ISBN 978-1-78088-025-9

British Library Cataloguing in Publication Data.
A catalogue record for this book is available from the British Library.

Layout: suesmith@roseweek.com
Cover design: ElburyDesign.com
Cover photo: John Such @ SuchGoodPictures.co.uk
Karate support from Gary Roberts and Paul Craig of the TSKA
www.davidcroft.info

Matador is an imprint of Troubador Publishing Ltd

Printed and bound by TJ International Ltd, Padstow, Cornwall

Also supporting:

Hospitality Action and Regain will each receive £1 from the sale of every book

Foreword

Having not had any contact with David for over 25 years, I was more than pleased to be asked to write a piece for his book. I first became aware of David when he attended the last of the British Karate Association's Summer Courses in the early 1970s, when the BKA was the main governing body for karate in Great Britain. His enthusiasm, like that of many others, shone through during the week and cemented his desire to learn more. This enthusiasm became more apparent to me when he travelled all the way from Cornwall as one of the youngest students to attend the first course I held in London in conjunction with Dominic Valera. I was also a member of the grading panel when David achieved his 1st Dan under the BKA. After this he went on to become a prominent member of John Smith's Bujinkai Karate Association, fighting on two occasions in the British Championships at Crystal Palace. However, my overriding memories of David are of when he worked in London. Despite failing to find accommodation near my club in Dagenham,

he still travelled from the other side of London on many evenings to train after work. This was a golden era for my Ishinryu Karate Association and the England team, with many of my students and other visiting students making up the England squad. David was therefore able to compete with some of the best in the world and, again, his enthusiasm was always evident. As he mentions in this book, he was on the verge of being chosen for the England under-21 squad. Had he not gone abroad to work I'm sure he would have achieved this goal. It therefore came as no surprise to me and to others in the karate community when we heard that he would represent Bermuda in the 1980 WUKO world championships and inaugural World Games. It was at these events, I assumed, that I would meet up with David next. However, his accident dealt a devastating blow, and the next time I was to see him was when, with friends, he attended the British Championships in Birmingham. Despite not having much time to spare due to coaching, I managed a brief chat with him and was amazed at how cheerful he remained despite being in a wheelchair and having to cope with the other consequences and difficulties associated with his accident. In view of his fighting spirit before the accident, it came as no surprise to me to read of all the things he has achieved over the years. Sustaining a spinal cord injury is a life-changing event, and while the karate community gave some support to help David overcome his initial difficulties, I am pleased that he has been able to find support elsewhere through the intervening years. I therefore hope the various karate associa-

tions, their members and the wider martial arts community purchase copies of this book. I feel that David's story is a great read, demonstrating not only his own achievements but also the achievements of others who have sustained a spinal cord injury in a sporting accident. The cookbook section has some great recipes – who knows, I might even try one or two of them myself!

Ticky

Ticky Donovan

OBE 9th Dan

Contents

Introduction

I have often been told that I should write a book about my life experiences, as, no doubt, have many others, both disabled and able bodied. The practicalities of such a project, however, were daunting. English was not my best subject at school and I believe that, compared with some people, I have really done nothing particularly extraordinary with my life. These factors, combined with other difficulties I have had in my life, made the prospect too difficult to contemplate. When I did, finally, first consider this book and its introduction, I did not want it to be a 'warts and all' confessional, as seems to be the trend nowadays. There are certain things in my life which I cannot get closure on and others which I feel should be kept private, so some areas have been left deliberately vague. Similarly, I felt it right only to mention people by name in order to explain certain encounters. I hope that this introduction, though slightly different from others, gives a well-balanced insight into my life, including my time in the hospitality industry, some of my time being disabled and my time doing karate.

After breaking my neck I was gravely ill, and at that time food and eating did not seem important; even as I got better it was difficult for others to get me to eat. This was mostly due to my not having much of an appetite. I was not only trying to come to terms with the consequences of my accident, but my liking for particular foods at that time was limited. Even so, as my condition improved at the spinal unit, food was to play an important part in my life and in the lives of other people. With the food at the unit being occasionally rather bland, the highlight of the week would often be when relatives brought in home-cooked treats, or when we ordered in from outside. The highlight of the week's offerings of hospital food would often be the roast dinners. These were always good hearty meals, especially welcome after gruelling physiotherapy sessions or a few beers at the weekend. With about 15 people in wheelchairs to be accommodated at one long table, and with people jostling to get a good place and a hot meal, such occasions would often resemble a scene from Ben Hur! On top of this, some patients had no or very limited hand movement, so some would need their food cut up and others would have to be fed. Those with very limited movement would often leave food, frustrated at not being able to cut it up. The same sort of thing would also happen when eating out during an 'escape session' from the hospital with staff, friends or loved ones. After I returned home to live, going out for a meal would often mean either someone would have to cut up my food for me or I would choose something from the menu which didn't need cutting up – even if was not particularly what I wanted. Romantic meals out were also sometimes a bit of a disaster, as my companion, in reaching over to cut up my dinner, could hardly avoid getting her sleeves dirty in her own plate of food! While this was going on, her own meal would more than likely go cold.

On one romantic meal out at a really nice restaurant a few years after my accident, châteaubriand (a fillet steak for two carved at the table) was on the menu, and I thought, 'Brilliant! I've got this one sorted! When the waiter asked what I would like I said, 'Châteaubriand, please,' knowing my guest would enjoy it as much as I did. My guest then told the waiter that she would have the same, at which he had to explain that one steak was a meal for two and we ended up in hysterics. Not only did my food have no bones in it, but it was cut up by the waiter, which made for an extremely enjoyable evening. Not long after this began the craze for nouvelle cuisine, and what should have been a beautifully presented meal could end up looking as if it had been thrown against a wall after being cut up. Even at Hotelympia, or when I was invited to the odd charity dinner at which some of the best chefs in the world would cook superb food, it would often still need to be cut up for me, or for anyone else in my situation. It is because of this situation

that I decided to get the chefs who have contributed to this book to try and present food in a way that would be user-friendly to someone with limited dexterity. In answer to those who have asked why I have not featured meals that can be prepared easily by disabled people, my point is that, while some tetraplegics are able to cook meals, many with limited dexterity or no hand movement are not able to do so. There are already cookbooks on the market that contain simple-to-prepare meals that can be cooked by a disabled people, their loved ones or PA/carers, some of which I use myself. I have had many PA/carers from many countries. Some of them have just left home with their cooking skills ranging from basic to competent. Also, some of them have had limited interest in cooking and in some cases only a basic grasp of the English language and food hygiene, so at times my house can be like a cookery school and language school combined, with me having to have the patience of a saint! Such a cookbook, though it would possibly be extremely funny in places, would require a very long introduction indeed, due to the many and varied misunderstandings that have occurred over the years! Similarly, while I consider that I was an extremely competent pastry chef at the time of my accident, my general cooking skills have been matched and even bettered by some of the more mature PA/carers. So while this book may not be a panacea for all, I hope that those who have disabilities, and others, will find many of the recipes easy to cook. I also hope that through this book chefs, and others in the hospitality industry, can gain a better understanding of those problems faced by disabled people that may not have been considered in other cookery books.

In respect of my life, I was born in Romford, Essex, where we lived for two years until our family had to move to Ballykelly in Northern Ireland as my father was a Navigator in the RAF. After three years, my father having been made up to the rank of Squadron Leader, we were posted to RAF St Mawgan, near Newquay, Cornwall, and we lived nearby at St Eval. While at St Mawgan, during a ceremony at which the Queen and the Duke of Edinburgh were awarding the squadron standard, it was obvious that my father's marching was not as it should be and, at the age of 35, he was diagnosed with Parkinson's disease and given a medical discharge.

As a family we were then fortunate to be able to move to a house overlooking Mawgan Porth beach, thanks in part to the support of the RAF Benevolent Fund. Most of my childhood was therefore spent swimming, surfing, diving and fishing and most of my younger years doing various sports – I was

As a carefree two-year-old.

chosen to represent the junior school at football as well becoming Cornwall swimming and diving champion at junior school level. To supplement my income I, along with others, used to collect Coke bottles from rubbish bins and claim the money back on them, as well as working in local cafés and restaurants. We would also find lost coins and other items on the beach – no metal detectors back then! The odd trout or salmon caught under the lock gates on the river also earned us a few extra bob, until the water bailiffs put a stop to it. Although my father was unable to drive due to his illness, one of the volunteer drivers from the local hospital used to take us to local football matches, and I also got to see an England under-23 International against Bulgaria at Home Park, Plymouth. This had me hooked on Plymouth Argyle, and when I was slightly older and was allowed on many occasions to go on the train to watch them play, my friends and I had some crazy adventures. This period coincided with Argyle's dream season, when they gained promotion thanks to the efforts of such players as Paul Mariner and Billy Rafferty. Luckily for me, while also still a teenager a karate club opened in the village. This was before the boom in martial arts following the Bruce Lee films, and the

Doing a Yoko Geri Jodan (karate side kick) at the age of 15.

training, although very hard, was also extremely rewarding. I found myself rising up the grades and eventually obtained my Dan grade.

My options after leaving school were rather limited, as Cornwall at the time was mostly dependent on the hospitality and china clay industries. As a result, I was advised to train as a chef, as, apart from sport, cooking was one of my other interests and one of my better subjects at school. Along with 10 other hopefuls, I went for an interview only to find it had been cancelled as it was the head chef's day off. As I was the only one who bothered to turn up the following day, I got the job and entered the hospitality industry at the Hotel Bristol in Newquay. This I found enjoyable enough, as I was eventually able to live in and be central to every-

thing and close to friends. However, I soon found that the long hours affected my social activities – especially my chances to make it into the England karate squad – as I worked most weekends and evenings. I spent nearly two years at the hotel and, as I was often used as the whipping-boy, so to speak – given the most mundane tasks and not taught much – I kept looking out for a more suitable job. Luckily, I then got a letter offering me a job with the Savoy Group at Stone's Chop House, their English restaurant in Piccadilly, which was very similar to the Savoy's Simpson's in the Strand. So, at the age of 18, off I went to London, where I stayed at a hostel in Holland Park owned by the Savoy.

My social life in London, though I was away from home and loved ones, was better in some respects, as we did straight shifts and had every other weekend off. I was therefore able to do more karate and even train with members of the England squad. I spent six months at Stone's and enjoyed my time there, but when my father sadly died I felt I needed a fresh environment and went for a job at the Savoy Grill. Despite there being no vacancies at the time, I was given a job by the sous chef, who thought I had shown a lot of tenacity in going to the Grill kitchen for a job as opposed to the other restaurants in the Savoy Group.

Life in the Grill kitchen proved quite a culture shock at first, as virtually all the menus and orders were in French, and the standard of cooking was much higher than anything I was used to. I wanted to work in the pastry department, as this was what I knew most about and enjoyed the most, but I ended up spending two months on the soup section followed by two months on the veg section and another two months on the roast section. The latter happened around the Glorious Twelfth, when the Savoy usually won the race to have the first grouse shot in Scotland flown to London, cooked and on the table. Service was really manic at such times, with orders coming in left, right and centre for grouse, partridge and pheasant, as well as for the roasts normally on offer. On one particular day service was hectic, and the sous chef was going ballistic trying to get everything out on time. He was not the most pleasant person at times and used to call everyone 'boo boo', together with a lot of other verbal abuse. Things came to a head when I was carrying a pheasant on a large silver salver and the sous chef, not knowing that my father had recently died, said, 'Come on, boo boo, what your father teach you?' Well, this was the straw that broke the camel's back. The silver salver went hurtling towards the sous chef, with pheasant, trimmings and gravy showering some of the other chefs. I charged towards the sous chef and was in the air, ready to do a flying sidekick to try and take him out. Luckily for him, and possibly for me, four of the other chefs saw what was coming and pinned me to the floor in mid-flight and in tears. Needless to say, the next day I thought it best to hand in my notice to the executive chef, who, by the way, was a lovely man. I went home to Cornwall, but when I returned to London a week later to get my belongings I heard that the day before, one of the other chefs, who had also been given a lot of verbal abuse, had chinned the sous chef, so in some respects justice was served!

My next job was at the Bedruthan Steps Hotel, which was just above our family home. I was given the job of head pastry chef, which I was really pleased about. The hotel was mainly for families and had superb facilities which the staff were fortunately also able to use. The food at the hotel at that time was not up to the standard I had become used to, and the menu, although changing on alternate weeks, was the same throughout the season. This meant I was able to improve many of the dishes and desserts, but was back doing split shifts and long hours. As I wanted to try and do straight shifts and more karate and be closer to my girlfriend, I got a job at the Headland Hotel in Newquay. The job there only lasted a week, as I then got coaxed back to the Bedruthan Steps on nearly double the money I was on previously. The hotel at that time was only open in the summer so at the end of the season I decided to return to London to get more experience.

I saw in *Caterer & Hotelkeeper* that the Churchill Hotel in London (*now Hyatt*

Regency London – The Churchill) was looking for a commis pastry chef. This was around the time that Norman Tebbit was urging everyone to get 'on your bike' and get a job, as unemployment was very high. Not only did I get free rail travel to London for the interview, but I managed to get the job with very good wages and was also able to get 'disturbance allowance' of £14 per week which, as part of the campaign, was to help people to move to a new location, so all in all life promised to be good. Unfortunately, like so many others moving to London, I found it difficult to find suitable accommodation and ended up sleeping on the floor of a flat rented by friends before finding a bedsit in a rather unpleasant shared house in Hammersmith. As this was not far from Loftus Road, I often went to see QPR play, as well as Chelsea at Stamford Bridge.

Working at the Churchill was absolutely superb. I learnt so much, and the executive chef and head pastry chef were great people. The camaraderie among the chefs was also really super, and everyone at the Churchill seemed to be treated as an equal no matter what position they held. While working at the Churchill, as I had at the Savoy, I used to do casual work for Ring & Brymer (*now Chester Boyd*) at their main kitchen in the City of London to top up my wages for weekends home. I was able to work for Ring & Brymer at numerous venues, including the Mansion House, the Guildhall, Armourers' Hall and HMS *Belfast*, jobs that would often turn out to be interesting. Whilst at the Churchill I was also able do to more karate than previously due to the kindness of the head pastry chef. This enabled me to train again with members of the England squad. As I also trained on occasions with a karate club in Ealing, I was also chosen to represent the borough in the London Borough Youth Games, and we gained the team bronze medal, narrowly missing out on the gold when we met Barking in the semi finals. Ironically, I did most of my training with members of the Barking team, and I won my fight, beating a current England under-21 team member and a future world team champion. At the time I had recently obtained my 2nd Dan, and the national coach was also considering me for a place in the England under-21 squad.

Though life was being kind to me, I had never had a holiday abroad in my life and had a desire to work overseas. With the blessing of the executive chef, I joined various agencies and had offers of jobs as head pastry chef in Syria, Bahrain and Saudi Arabia. However, I really wanted to work on an island and, having just missed out on a job in the Seychelles, I took a job as a demi pastry chef via VIP International at the Bermudiana Hotel in Bermuda, which was then part of Trusthouse Forte hotels. The contract, which would be for a year, included air tickets and accommodation. Not only

THE CHURCHILL

EXECUTIVE OFFICES
EB/rak

13th November 1979

TO WHOM IT MAY CONCERN

David CROFT

This is to confirm that the above mentioned person has been employed in my kitchen as a Pastry Commis since 13th November 1978.

He is an extremely capable chef with a great deal of flair and professional ability. He always carries out his duties to the best of his ability and to my entire satisfaction. His timekeeping attendance and reliability are very good and he is popular with all his colleagues.

David wishes now to extend his experience by working abroad and although I shall be sorry to lose him, I wish him success in his future career.

I can recommend him very highly to any future employer.

Edmond Beaufort
Executive Chef

THE CHURCHILL PORTMAN SQUARE LONDON, W1H OAJ ENGLAND
TELEPHONE: 01-486 5800   TELEX: 264831

A LOEWS HOTEL

Loews (GB) Ltd, 11 Mansfield St, London W1 Reg. 922947 Isidore Kerman Gordon Webb (UK) Laurence A Tisch Preston R Tisch Lester Pollack Robert J Hausman Roy E Posner B Hirsch that, but Bermuda was a tax-free island! This felt like a dream job to me at the time, and though I would miss friends and loved ones, it also seemed like an ideal career progression.

I flew out to Bermuda at the age of 20 on the day before Christmas Eve and was thrown in at the deep end, so to speak, by the head pastry chef so he could have Christmas off! The job, though, turned out to be pretty mundane.

Overlooking Hamilton Harbour, two days after arriving in Bermuda.

There was the same two-weekly menu which found me mostly making chocolate cakes and apple pies for American tourists. However, it was fantastic in so many other areas. I was again doing split shifts, but as the hotel only really concentrated on dinner, we could be finished by 12pm on the early shift and by 8pm on the late shift. Most afternoons were spent at the superb Horseshoe Bay sunbathing, swimming, diving and snorkelling, with most evenings spent in the staff bar, pubs and disco. On other evenings and on my days off I used to train with the local karate club. I was able to meet up with friends and go sightseeing, go to Sunday brunches and beach parties, as well as do other sports. The people of Bermuda were so friendly and life there was so laid-back that it was an idyllic time.

Six months into my contract and three months after my 21st birthday, during a training session with the local karate club, who were in training for the 1980 WUKO world championships in Madrid and forthcoming world games in Santa Clara,

Rather smashed on a booze cruise in Bermuda.

California, I was told I would be included in the team representing Bermuda at both tournaments, most of our costs being met by various fundraising events. Those of us who were to be included in the team were so overjoyed we did some extra and exhausting training that morning. I then got on my moped (the usual form of transport in Bermuda) and rode to Horseshoe Bay to meet up with friends. As we were relaxing, some of my friends said, 'Let's go diving.' This was usually done off a rock about 50 yards out to sea and into deep water. However, because I was still tired I just wanted to chill out. I was then told about a new cove where everyone had gone diving the day before, so we all went along to have a look. I checked the depth of the water – it was only about six feet deep – and followed my friend to the top of the rock they had dived off the previous day, which was about 30 feet high. I told my friend he was crazy to dive from such a height, but he jumped into the water with no problems and then climbed back up to the top of the rock and jumped off again with no problems. As I was not keen to jump from 30 feet, I came down to a height I thought would be safe to dive from – about six feet. When I dived into the water my head hit the sea bed with an almighty bang, resulting in a complete loss of feeling from the neck down, and I was left floating motionless in the water. The ironic thing was that although I had done some crazy things in my life, I had never broken a single bone in my body, and yet my moment of caution was to have devastating consequences.

I was unable to move or take a breath. What if my friends thought I was playing a practical joke? Thankfully, they realised what had happened and got me out of the water just in time and then back to the beach. I remember asking to be turned on my back. I then said my feet were in the air, and when I was told that they were not it sank in that my accident must be serious. Strangely, not knowing what was ahead of me, I recall saying to my friends to switch the machine off when I got to the hospital – not that I would necessarily be put on a life-support machine. Within a short while a nurse and paramedic arrived and I was asked if I could feel my body, to which I replied no, except that I could feel a bit of stiffness in a rather important area, which seemed to amuse and bemuse everyone, including the doctors in casualty later!

I was taken to the main hospital on the island and on arrival was asked if I had any medical insurance. Thankfully, we had to have insurance as a condition of our employment, as my medical bills would eventually amount to £13,000, and what this would equate to 30 years on I dread to think. A doctor then examined me and again I was asked if I could feel my body and again I had to say no. I recall the doctor then saying to my friend, 'You do realise that this is very serious?' I can't remember much after that until I woke up in a bright room and heard a crunching noise as a doctor appeared to be drilling into my head. This was so they could apply skull traction to try and alleviate some of the damage to my spinal cord and straighten my broken neck, as I had apparently broken it at the 4th cervical level with associated C4/5 fracture dislocation. After this I was taken to the intensive care unit.

The next few days were rather hazy and on the fourth day my stomach blew up like a pregnant woman's overnight and I was diagnosed with a duodenal stress ulcer. I was rushed to the operating theatre for emergency surgery and a tracheotomy tube was inserted into my throat. I was then put on a ventilator, with drips and tubes inserted all over my body. Upon my return from the operating theatre I would be fighting for my life, as it was thought unlikely that I would survive the next 48 hours. Had I not been so fit from doing karate and other sports, the eventual outcome could have been completely different. I was very fortunate indeed that I already knew some of the nurses in ICU, as some were expats or friends of my workmates whom I had met previously. Whether the treatment I was given avoided later complications I do not know, but I could not have had better care had I been royalty.

Likewise, I was fortunate that some of my family were able to fly out to Bermuda, along with the girl I had been going out with at home, whose mother

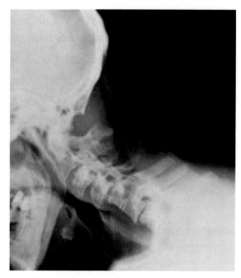

An X ray showing fracture dislocation at C4/5 vertebral bodies.

very kindly funded her flight from Cornwall. All this support was very uplifting. Similarly, the doctors were wonderful, and let many of my friends visit on most days to keep my spirits up. Even now I find it hard to recollect my first few days in ICU, as I was on some very powerful drugs to keep me sedated and was apparently saying some rather bizarre things. There was one rather strange moment when I thought I was at a football match. I could hear lots of cheering and clapping and thought someone had scored a goal.

I was told by one of the nurses that I was getting better. I was so befuddled that when one of my relatives told me there was really good news, I had opened my bowels, I frowned, thinking, 'What the hell are bowels?' My girlfriend was then told to explain things to me a bit more simply! Still not able to get my head around things, I thought, 'Christ, the jungle drums will be going around big time on this news and I'll have to lie low for a few weeks and not be able to go to the pub or disco.'

The most horrendous part of being in ICU, besides the paralysis and not being able to speak, was that I was on a Stryker frame. This can only be described as a big padded ironing board with a metal frame surrounding it. Every few hours, pillows would be put on top of my body followed by another padded ironing board and the whole thing would be turned over so I was lying face down, looking at the floor. This was to relieve pressure on my back. The whole process of being turned was agonising not only for me but for everyone else as well. Despite being paralysed from the neck down, unable to speak and surrounded with monitors and drips, I remember one hilarious moment. An older women, a friend of one my workmates, used to come into ICU to read to me. One day she told me that she had met some of my other friends in the pub

and that she had gone back to one lad's apartment for coffee. When the lads came into ICU later in the day, they were thrown into a panic as they found me laughing, crying and gasping for breath all at the same time and no one could figure out what was wrong. The nurses were

also completely puzzled and concerned. I had put two and two together and when I tried to mouth the lady's name no one could understand what I was saying as I was using her nickname. When everyone finally figured out what I was trying to say, my friend was none too pleased, as he had told them he had taken a really posh, cracking looking girl back to his flat that afternoon and everyone now knew differently!

A few days after this incident the doctors were thankfully able to get a mechanical voice box from America to go onto the tracheotomy tube. Though it was great to be able to speak, it made me sound like Mickey Mouse. One day, about three weeks later, I was lying face down on the Stryker frame when I thought, 'Blimey, that seems unusual!' Some slight sensation had returned to my body while a nurse was taking my temperature 'veterinary style'. While this was good news in many respects, as later on I would know when I needed assistance with bodily functions and would be aware of

The end of the turning process while encased in a Stryker frame before the top section of the frame is removed to allow you to lie face down (photograph from Life *magazine).*

where my body was positioned, I began to feel a great deal of pain and had muscle spasms which were hard to control and caused many additional problems.

I spent most days in ICU inundated with friends visiting, being read cards and letters sent from back home and from numerous people I did not even know, many of which used to have me in tears at the kindness of the things being written. I would also have physiotherapy sessions to try and relieve the muscle spasms and combat the various contractures of my hands that were starting. While I was in ICU my friends also held various fundraising events to help with my repatriation, as such costs were bizarrely not covered by my health insurance. The flight to get me back to England would require British Airways to remove six seats from the plane to make room for a stretcher. Return tickets for a doctor and a nurse would also have to be paid for – all in all it would cost over £3,000. I would spend a total of six weeks in ICU before being flown back to England to be rehabilitated at the National Spinal Injuries Centre at Stoke Mandeville Hospital.

During the rest of my time in ICU, the nurses and doctors tried to get me used to the idea that I would probably be paralysed for the rest of my life, although I was never really told this. To try and give me a better insight into how life as a quadriplegic might be I was given to read an autobiography by Joni Eareckson, an American girl who, some years earlier, had also broken her neck in a diving accident. After her accident Joni had become an artist and produced superb paintings using just her mouth to hold a pencil or paint brush. However, I believe she was of the opinion that she was meant to be in a wheelchair, as she had sinned in a cornfield with her boyfriend, and that this would better enable her to preach the word of God in the future. The nurses often used to say to me, 'You haven't read much more of the book, David.' I think I replied one day that if she thought she should be in a wheelchair due to sinning in a cornfield then I should be sprayed with some holy water! The book never came back for me to read any more of it!

During the final few days before I returned to England, the medical staff tried to lift my spirits by explaining that I would be going to one of the best spinal units in the world and that they could do incredible things. I still couldn't get my head around everything. My life still revolved around being turned every few hours on the Stryker frame and having my tracheotomy suctioned regularly, and there was little improvement in my condition. My last days in ICU were mostly spent with people popping in to say their goodbyes. These were very emotional times, as I knew I might never see some of these people again. The general manager of the hotel also came in to wish me well in the future. This, combined with my contract being cancelled and my friends informing me that VIP International had another chef on the way to replace me, seemed to signal the end of my career in the hospitality industry and, in turn, any support from or involvement with the industry in the future.

I was fortunate that I could choose one of the nurses I knew to accompany me on the flight to Heathrow and onwards to Stoke Mandeville Hospital. On the day of departure the nurse and accompanying doctor prepared all the medication that would be needed for the long flight back to England. At that time I was still on a lot of morphine-based and other muscle-relaxing drugs. I also still had various IV drips inserted, and my tracheotomy tube, which still had to be suctioned every few hours. My departure from the island therefore contrasted somewhat with my arrival there six months earlier.

At the airport I was taken out of the ambulance and, though I was able to see some of the outside world for the first time in six weeks, I was sort of smuggled into the back of the aeroplane and placed on a stretcher which appeared to be part of the luggage rack, so not exactly the sort of thing you see in holiday brochures. The flight home would take about eight hours and, as it was at night, I spent most of the time trying to sleep. This was virtually impossible, however, as the bung in my tracheotomy tube kept popping out every half an hour or so due to the cabin pressure.

On arrival at Heathrow we were taken to the medical section and then on to Stoke Mandeville Hospital by ambulance – a journey made at 20 miles per hour to avoid any vibration affecting my still somewhat unstable broken neck. On arrival at Stoke Mandeville it came as something of a culture shock that I had to wait in the corridor for about three hours before being seen by a doctor. I then saw the spinal consultant and his senior houseman, both of whom examined me with pins and cotton wool to see what level of sensation and movement I had. Most of the talk at the time was complete gobbledegook to me. After the examination I was transferred from the ambulance trolley to a mechanical bed as opposed to the dreaded Stryker frame, which was a great relief. Then all the IV drips were taken out and I was told I would not be given any more morphine-based drugs. I was also given a name badge above my bed with 'C4/5' written below it, which, I was told, was my lesion level. I was also told that I was tetraplegic, as opposed to the America term quadriplegic, which had me even more confused. Although the terminology is different, the diagnosis is the same, as all four limbs are affected. I do not remember much more of that day until the evening, when I was woken up by many of the other patients talking to each other and making a lot of noise. Then the guy nearest to me started to play a harmonica and I thought, 'All he needs to do now is play the last post and I'll be taken away in a coffin.' The place seemed like a complete and utter madhouse compared to my time in ICU in Bermuda.

The following day I was a bit more aware of my surroundings and met some of the nurses and care staff who would be involved in my rehabilitation. I also started to become more aware of some of the other patients, especially those who were closest to my bed. The guy next to me, who had broken his neck in a diving accident in Gibraltar, was a right character, and another guy on the other side of the ward, who had broken his back falling off a ladder, appeared a total nutcase. Both, though, would be good talking buddies for the next few weeks, as we were all lying flat on our backs. Later that day the doctors and nurses visited to assess my condition and, due to a pressure sore above my bottom, I was told that I would have to spend at least three months in bed. This meant that I would probably spend the same amount of time in bed as some of the other newly injured patients.

Most mornings were devoted to toilet routines, being washed by nurses or nursing auxiliaries and having my tracheotomy and pressure sore attended to. I would also have occupational and physiotherapy sessions, most of which concentrated on trying to deal with my severe muscle spasms and the contractures of my hands and legs. A strange thing that used to happen in the mornings was that I would hear a whirring noise – when you are lying on your back and can only see the ceiling your mind can play some strange tricks on you. Each morning I would hear the same noise, similar to an electric drill, so I thought that it must be a new patient having skull traction fitted. I later found out that the noise was, in fact, one of the cleaners using an electric buffer to clean the floors! My three months in bed were spent getting to know other patients and being visited by friends and family.

Within three months my pressure sore had thankfully healed. The tracheotomy tube was removed and the wound healed over but left a very ugly looking scar in the middle of my neck. I was still suffering a great deal of pain and muscle spasms, both of which I found more debilitating than the paralysis at times – and the same can still apply to this day. I constantly asked the consultant if anything could be done to help me, but all he did was ask what the surf was going to be like in Cornwall, as he sometimes stayed at the hotel above our family home and went surfing from the beach! You soon came to realise that you had to put up with things while cocktails of medications were tried out on you. These could have both good and bad effects. I recall being put on steroids at one stage but soon asked to be taken off them – the thought of being in a wheelchair with developing breasts was not very appealing!

On my ward there were approximately

24 other people suffering varying degrees of spinal injury from a variety of causes. Most had resulted from road traffic accidents, followed by rugby, swimming and diving accidents. There were also those who had been injured falling off ladders or who had had other work related accidents. The rest had been paralysed in other ways – one had been stabbed, one had a spinal infection and another was paralysed as the result of a medical blunder. One chap said he had fallen out of a window, but we later found out he had had to jump out of the window when his lady-friend's husband had come home early. This had us all aching with laughter the night the truth came out.

At Stoke Mandeville Hospital four months after my accident.

I would end up spending a total of 11 months at Stoke Mandeville and felt extremely fortunate to have been treated in a spinal unit, where the knowledge you gained about your condition was second to none. The wards were sort of split up into three sections. The first section was for those who were newly injured and still in bed, while the middle section was made up of people starting to get up and getting used to being in a wheelchair or trying to walk again. The final section was for those either close to going home, leaving for other hospitals or going to other types of accommodation. It was from the people in the latter section that you could usually glean information as to what may lie ahead with your rehabilitation. Similarly, you would try and find out about the tests and operations that were ahead of you, and sometimes someone would give you a totally different idea of what was ahead to try and wind you up. Such humour and camaraderie, while they lifted the spirits of everyone else, at the same time could make the person awaiting a test or operation feel much more anxious than they needed to be.

The camaraderie throughout the whole 11 months was amazing, especially when former patients who came back for check-ups would explain some of the things they were able to do back in the outside world. During my time at the spinal unit, myself and others would be shown how best to make use of the movement we had left, or how to develop it further. On weekdays we were always busy learning new things, and in the evenings we were sometimes able to go with nurses or physios or the family and friends of other patients to the nearby sports centre. These occasions were always great, as we usually ended up managing to get pretty drunk and swap various theories on how we thought our rehabilitation was going. These escape sessions would often allow patients to get better acquainted with the staff, and relationships would sometimes be struck up.

During my time in the hospital, family, friends and loved ones did visit, but the distances involved and the cost of travelling from Cornwall and elsewhere made it difficult. Near the end of my time at the hospital most of the patients who lived not too far away were able to go home for weekends. However, this was not practical for me and two of the other patients, so our weekends were spent gambling and drinking until we realised that we had better prepare more sensibly for the future. During our rehabilitation process we were advised to try and think about what we might do once we left the hospital. This was easy for those who could continue with their college or university courses or who had academic careers. Those who had served in the Forces also seemed to get more support, as they often had visits from rehabilitation officers and career advisors, while for others there was the possibility of compensation

from their accident. Likewise, if you were injured in certain sports, you also seemed to get a great deal of support.

All I and others like me could do was try and get our heads around what it would be like living life day to day. Even though I had been working for one of the largest hotel chains in the world at the time of my accident, the last contact I had had with the hospitality industry was a good luck message from the general manager as I was leaving ICU in Bermuda. One thing you soon learned was that without the possibility of compensation, without good family or other support, it was a case of sink or swim in the outside world.

I was fortunate in some respects, as the plan was that I would go back to my family home, where a small extension would be built as fit as possible for my needs. However, this would take many months, and in the meantime I would be spending most of my time in the inaccessible environment of a back bedroom, which would not be easy for me or for others. Friends would visit occasionally and, even though it was not easy getting out of the house, I was taken on some crazy adventures.

One friend – one of the village characters – was likely to turn up in a different car each time he took me out. On one occasion, not only was there no seatbelt but the door was half hanging off, and I seem to recall being strapped into the seat with binder twine. On another occasion we went out promising to be back by

11pm but ended up in a nightclub till about 2am, myself and my wheelchair having been lifted by my doorman friends in and out of pubs, most of which were otherwise inaccessible to me. On arriving home, both of us rather the worse for wear, I told my friend he would have to put me to bed, as my family would have been none too pleased at being woken up at this late hour. Having not put me in bed before, my friend tried to do what had to be done, but in his haste things got a bit muddled and everything went a bit haywire.

'Christ, I need a pee!' I said. 'Hurry up – with all the beer I've drunk the bed could be like a pond.' In a panic he grabbed a potted plant off the table, pulled the plant out of the pot, shoved the pot between my legs and said, 'The plant needs watering.'

This had us both aching with laughter and, to top it all, the phone then rang, waking everyone in the house. It was my friend's girlfriend trying to track him down. With no one particularly happy about being woken up at such an hour, my friend was given his marching orders and I was more or less told that I was grounded for a while. After this I spent approximately three more months in the back bedroom with little chance of getting out, as the house was still not very wheelchair accessible. It was then decided that I should go to my nearest general hospital in Truro until the building works could be completed.

I spent approximately six months at the hospital on an orthopaedic ward where many of the patients were young and in leg traction following motorcycle accidents. This, combined with the fact that many of the nurses were my own age and that I was also able to do hydrotherapy and occupational therapy, gave my life a bit of reality again. At the time I also had a friend who ran a hotel in Truro, so I was able to go there at weekends and sometimes in the evening.

These were great times, as I could sit in the bar talking to people and eating lovely home-cooked food, as well as having the odd card session. During the evening visits, the ward sister used to let me stay out till about 9pm so the night staff could then give me a hand to get to bed. As time went by we ended up going back later and later, as everyone felt it was good for me to enjoy myself and turned a blind eye to things. One evening we arrived back so late that the hospital doors were locked and we had to go in through the casualty department. Lots of people rushed to see if I was OK, at which point, I believe, I said, 'Great, thanks. I just need to get some sleep.'

The next day the ward sister said she had heard that there was a bit of a disturbance in casualty the night before, and asked was I involved. I protested my innocence while the other nurses stood around with wry smiles on their faces. Following this it was agreed that I could stay the weekend at my friend's hotel and he would get me up and put me to bed, often after late lock-ins in the hotel. We also had many other crazy times. Once, when my friend was pushing me around town, we went into WH Smith, where I was looking at various karate magazines and asked him to pass me one. At that time the movement in my arms was very limited, besides which I had a really heavy NHS wheelchair which I could hardly push. We used to play practical jokes on each other all the time, and my friend decided it was my turn again. He grabbed a *Playboy* magazine off the top shelf, opened it to the centre pages, put it on my lap and then ran out of the shop, leaving me unable to move the magazine and crying my eyes out with laughter as he waved at me from outside. At that point an old lady proceeded to look at some magazines and put her arm on my shoulder and said, 'It's all right dear, I understand.'

The modifications at home seemed to be continually delayed for various reasons and, as it was felt that I was using an NHS bed when it was not really necessary, it was decided that I should move to a local rehabilitation unit for young people. I was taken there to have a look around by the hospital social worker, and as the unit had people with varying degrees and different kinds of disability I asked if I could stay at the hospital for a little longer. This, though, was not possible, as the building work at home was still being delayed.

I was taken for another visit to the unit in the hospital's wheelchair-accessible mini-van, which was a bit like the Pope-mobile with me sitting up in the back. On the way back to the hospital we had to go to Newquay, where I was able to meet up with some friends in the pub. Knowing what they would make of the van, I asked if it could be parked round the back of the pub. The social worker, however, felt it was best to park outside the pub, whereupon one of my friends opened the door of the van and said, 'Two ice creams, please.' I didn't know whether to laugh or cry but, as usual, it had me laughing at the irony of the situation.

A few weeks later I moved to the rehabilitation unit and, though I was still reluctant at the time, it would prove to be a better environment than the local hospital. There was a very relaxed attitude to things, besides which everyone had their own room, and after a while I got a better understanding of some of the other residents' disabilities. I was also fortunate in that the landlady of one of the pubs in my home village at that time was able to get funding for an electric wheelchair for me, and this was topped up with some fundraising by my local karate association, along with others in the karate community. This gave me more freedom and enabled me to get to the local shops, which were not far away.

Most of the staff at the unit were really lovely, although such places always have some people you can never see eye-to-eye with, which can cause problems when you are dependent on them for assistance. Most of the residents would go home at weekends, so only myself and one or two other wheelchair users would be at the unit then. Most were fully independent, so I was fortunate that I could build up good relationships with some of the staff, and on many occasions we were able to go out in the minibus on day trips or to the pub, as well as to various concerts locally. My time there would only last a little longer, however, as the room being built onto my family home was nearing completion.

Returning to my family home nearly two and a half years after my accident came as a relief at first, but in time things deteriorated, as community and other care was very limited in those days and I had to go to bed at 9pm most evenings. Also, the family members I was living with were working long hours and now had a young baby, so their time was often taken up elsewhere. Though by then I had a Motability vehicle, in addition to which another pub in the village had very generously raised the funds for a wheelchair that could go in the front passenger seat of the car, the car itself was often being used by other family members, and Motability at that time only allowed two nominated drivers who could not be changed easily at short notice. Thankfully, though, around this time I had a visit from a representative of the Sequal Trust (formerly the Possum Users' Association),

Using the computer system supplied by the Sequal Trust.

who were able to provide me with one of the first Apple IIe computers, which had been kindly donated by Apple Computers to the Sequal Trust. I found it easier to use this instead of a traditional typewriter to keep in touch with people. I was also given a job by Cornwall County Council *(now Cornwall Council)* relaying messages for Minicom users. Although both of these gave me a greater purpose in life and I had a superb view overlooking Mawgan Porth beach, I felt a bit like a goldfish in a bowl, as I often couldn't get out of the house in winter and couldn't get out of the car park unaided, even in an electric wheelchair, because of the incline.

The girlfriend I was going out with before my accident would visit occasionally but was now working long hours completing her training as a nurse, and anyway, she had sort of moved on with her personal life. Her mother also used to visit when she was in the area, and they were both concerned, as were others, about my well-being and the way I was living but felt unable to say anything. Friends would also visit when possible, but such visits were often limited, as most of them now had young families or were working long hours, while others had moved away.

It was decided that I should visit the rehabilitation centre for respite breaks to boost my morale and improve my social life. These visits were always a welcome relief, as I could meet up with some of the staff and residents, whom I got on well with, and have a reasonable social life. After a time I looked forward to these breaks more than ever, as I had struck up a special relationship with one of the care staff. She would occasionally visit me at home and could see the fragility of my situation. While our relationship became stronger over time, my health was deteriorating in certain respects, with many people now extremely concerned for my well-being. The rehabilitation centre management and others then decided that I was never going to make it out in the community if my visits there continued.

Fortunately, the staff member and I both found ourselves at a crossroads in life and, as we had much in common in different ways, so our friendship became even stronger. It was love in the true and real sense of things, and, while it was true she was now living on her own, I suppose the words 'Can I come and live with you?' were not the best sort of pro-posal. Thankfully, I was not told to get on my bike, and with our joint resources we looked into getting a mortgage and managed to purchase a small semi-detached bungalow. My partner also had two lovely teenage daughters, one of whom would live with us while the other would live nearby with her father.

Life was not easy, as my partner was my sole carer and mother to her daughters, as well as having to work part-time. We enjoyed the simple things in life at the time, and in many ways she was an angel from heaven, so to speak, as life at my family home would not have been sustainable in the long term.

I had by now acquired a new Motability vehicle which still required me to be transferred into the front seat of the car – not an easy task. While I now had the enjoyment of a true and loving family life, I also had the responsibility of making life easier for everyone, both now and in the future. I wrote to the personnel department at the Churchill Hotel to see if there was an industry charity, and in case this did not bring about a positive response I also wrote to the personnel department at Grosvenor House, this being one of the flagships of Trusthouse Forte hotels. I received a fantastic response from the executive chef at the Churchill, who said he would set up an appeal fund to get me a more suitable vehicle so I could travel without the need to be transferred. Similarly, my letter to Grosvenor House was forwarded to the Hotel and Catering

Benevolent Association (*now Hospitality Action*), whose chief executive sent me a very touching and supportive letter. After a few months, the Churchill's appeal was in full swing, with discos, fun runs and various other events being arranged, in addition to which, the sous chef planned to run the New York marathon on my behalf. The chief executive of the HCBA kept in continual contact and forwarded various letters in my name and, indeed, became a sort of father figure.

The Churchill's fundraising was thankfully absolutely exceptional, as adapted vehicles were not cheap and the HCBA had a capped limit on the support they could give. However, within a period of 18 months, enough money had been raised by all concerned to purchase the vehicle, and along the way I was asked to write an article for the HCBA's newsletter stating the purpose of the appeal along with my future goals. One of these was to take a holiday abroad, and I explained how difficult it was at the time to find

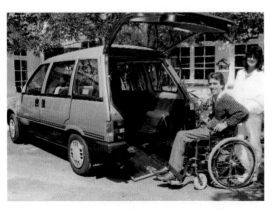

Adapted vehicle thanks to the support of the Churchill Hotel and HCBA (now Hospitality Action).

suitable accommodation for people in my situation, especially accommodation with wheel-in showers.

A few weeks later a letter arrived from the personnel director of Hilton International offering my partner and me a week's holiday at the Malta Hilton. This, combined with the new vehicle, seemed incredible. We therefore set off one day to go to the Churchill to meet many of the staff before flying out to Malta. I was informed that someone from the hotel would meet us at Paddington. I assumed this would be in a black cab, but, lo and behold, a chauffeur-driven stretch limousine, like something the Queen herself might use, was sent. While this was a lovely gesture in principle, trying to transfer me to the rear seat was impossible, so I was put in the front seat next to the chauffeur. The front seat was of the old-fashioned all-in-one variety, as well as being gleaming and highly polished. This, combined with the lack of seatbelt and my very poor balance, had me fighting to stay upright. As we turned the corner at Marble Arch, I had to say to the driver, 'Sorry, mate, nothing personal, but could you give my head a shove out of your groin and sit me upright, please?'

On arrival at the Churchill the executive chef, still his kindly, gracious self, greeted us, together with some of the management. We were then told there was a suite of rooms available for us to use along with a bottle of champagne, besides which I could meet up with some of my

Back in the pastry department at the Churchill with former colleagues.

another flight. On arriving back at Heathrow we were again met by a chauffeur-driven limousine and taken to the Churchill, where we met everyone again and were ribbed about missing the flight. Again we were invited to stay the night but unfortunately had train tickets booked. We were then dispatched in a black cab to Paddington with a box full of sandwiches and pastries for the journey home. The whole adventure kept us and everyone else at home amused and buoyed up for weeks, and it still holds fond memories to this day.

Following the holiday, the chief executive of the HCBA used to keep in regular contact and we even used to be sent a Christmas hamper, which was a lovely gesture, and this, combined with the paying of our television licence, was a great help. During the next year or so my health was still not at its best, mostly due to an underlying problem that had not been spotted locally. This all came to a head when I went for a check-up at Stoke Mandeville and, due to a urinary tract problem, was put on the emergency surgery list for the following day, much to my partner's concern. This would mean me having to stay in Stoke for three weeks and a further three weeks at an old hospital in Cornwall because, thanks to the local authority agreeing some improvements, there was building work going on at home with doors and windows boarded up and our small garden full of trenches, preventing access.

ex-colleagues, which was great. We were also told that we could eat anywhere in the hotel and were even invited to stay the night at the Churchill, which would have been superb. However, we had to decline as we had already been offered complimentary accommodation at the Copthorne Tara, one of the few really wheelchair-friendly hotels in London at the time.

The next day we flew out to Malta and had a wonderful, although not particularly easy, time, the hotel being not quite as user-friendly as we had been led to believe. However, we still managed to see quite a bit of the island, despite the difficulties – so much so, in fact, that we were enjoying a trip round the harbour when we should have been on our flight home! Thankfully, the general manager saw the funny side of things and allowed us to stay on at the hotel until we could get

On arriving home after the improvements it was great to have better access to the bungalow; it was also now more suitable for everyone and I had the space to take on various initiatives, most of them computer based. I also kept in contact with various ex-patients of Stoke Mandeville – one particular friend, who lived locally, had, ironically, broken his neck using the diving board at the hotel above the family home where I grew up, where I later worked. He had been training to be a chef at the time of his accident. He had slightly more movement than me and used to do superb printing from a garden shed using an old-style printing press, placing the type letter by letter to make up business cards, etc. His father, like mine, had served in the RAF and as they had known each other, his son used to keep me up to date with anything new. Around this time he informed me that another member of the RAF who had also been paralysed in an accident had set up a holiday trust for disabled RAF personnel. At the time non-dependants of ex-RAF personnel were also able to benefit, so me, my partner, her daughter and a friend of ours were able to enjoy a superb week's holiday at an apartment that the RAF had adapted in conjunction with the Holiday Property Bond in the Algarve, Portugal.

Although we now had a nice bungalow, things were never easy financially, and while I was aware that the HCBA were able to give weekly grants and the chief executive, I'm sure, would have been supportive of a request for such funding, at the time it didn't seem appropriate to ask – we had already been helped so much. Some months later I again had to go to Stoke for some minor operations to remove various cysts that had been causing problems for some time. Thankfully, during one of my spells in hospital one of the spinal consultants kindly arranged for the plastic surgery team to tidy up my tracheotomy scar. This, along with the other operations, would mean me staying in hospital for two weeks, which would prove beneficial in two ways. Firstly, the surgery on my tracheotomy scar was excellent and would allow me to wear opened-collared shirts in the future; secondly, I found out whilst talking to some of the other patients that most seemed to be getting more money per week than me. One of the patients kindly looked into matters more fully and discovered that I was missing out on some state funding. This came as a double whammy, as I had specifically asked a representative from the then Department of Social Security if I was getting all that I was entitled to and had been told 'Yes'.

On returning home I made inquiries again and was told that I was, in fact, being underpaid, and would now be paid the correct amount. On inquiring why this was not being backdated I was informed that the deciding officer deemed that this was not applicable but that I could appeal against the decision. One thing I have learned both from doing karate and from being in a spinal unit is that if you get a kick in the teeth, so to speak, then you should fight back and not throw in the towel. Putting in an appeal was like going into the unknown, as according to the paperwork my reasons for claiming back-dated payments did not appear valid. Thankfully, though, I had the support of a welfare rights unit that was available in Cornwall at that time.

Although unions were frowned upon within the hospitality industry, a union representative who lived not far away agreed to represent me at the appeal tribunal. This was a bit like the TV version of a crown court but less formal, and I wondered why the heck I was having to put up with all the garbage that was being put forward by the two representatives from the Department of Social Security *(now the Department of Work and Pensions)*. The union representative was able to put over my side of the case in an excellent way and when we returned to the room for the final decision the lay member of the panel winked at my partner and me. The chairman of the panel then informed us that my appeal was, in fact, valid and that everything would be backdated!

What a great relief. This would make life slightly easier for us and, with lightweight manual wheelchairs now available that were much easier to push and which allowed better posture than standard NHS wheelchairs, my partner suggested I use some of the money to buy one. While this was good news in some respects, as I was able to build up what few muscles I still had working, in other respects it would make me less independent in that my partner would again have to transfer me into our adapted vehicle. This would be slightly easier than before, and although it would still be a burden, she was prepared to do it for my sake.

At the time she was still working, and a combination of my past ill health, the fact that she suffered very bad migraines and the lack of community care at that time made us realise we should try and move to a property that would be more suitable in the event that a live-in PA/carer should be needed for respite care. Such a move would not be easy for various reasons, not the least of which was trying to find a property that was suitable, or could be made suitable, for a wheelchair user. We therefore put our bungalow on the market and quickly found a buyer for it. However, we had great difficulty finding a slightly bigger one within our price range. This process seemed to go on forever until we managed to find one which we thought could be adapted and made suitable for our future needs.

After moving in it soon became apparent that the cost of modifying and upgrading the bungalow would be vast, even with the assistance that was available from the local authority. We therefore decided not to do any modifications while we took stock of things. During this

On holiday in Majorca.

period we were offered another holiday in Majorca through the RAF trust, and again it was wonderful. Shortly afterwards, however, I was informed that due to demand, in future the RAF trust would only be able to offer holidays to RAF personnel.

As I was well aware that people in my position need a holiday, and having time on my hands, some friends and I decided to set up a similar trust for hospitality industry personnel. This would not be easy, as we had never done anything similar before. Likewise, there was now a new chief executive at the HCBA who was not as supportive as his predecessor. However, some fantastic prizes were donated by numerous hotels and restaurants for a national raffle, and somewhat madly but enthusiastically I took out a

loan for the printing of raffle tickets and put out a mailshot to virtually every hotel and restaurant in Great Britain. For a time you could hardly move in the bungalow for raffle tickets, letters and envelopes. Thankfully, this outlay proved a good investment, and I paid off the loan and some holiday provision was also made available. However, with the long-term objectives of the trust being to raise vast sums, all concerned made the decision later on to wind up the trust and offer the holiday provision to the HCBA.

Having now spent over a year in the bungalow under difficult circumstances, and with the housing market going crazy, with prices rising thousands in a matter of months, we decided to put the bungalow on the market and look for something more suitable for the future. Fortunately, a local couple came to see the bungalow and, though it was not suitable for them, they asked what our future plans were. We replied that ideally we would like to find a plot of land and build a property as suitable as possible for our future needs. The couple then left, saying they would see what they could do. About a week later the lady rang to ask us to give a friend of hers a call. This I did a week or so later and we got an invitation to visit a couple who lived in a hamlet not far from where we lived.

On arrival we were met by an older man and his wife who wanted to sell off part of their garden as a building plot. The man – a great character – was almost in tears when he first met me, and said he would be happy for us to live next door. Explaining that I was unable to raise a deposit as we had not yet sold our bungalow, I was told, 'It's all right, boy, the plot of land is yours when you're ready.'

After this visit we got an architect we knew to draw up plans, and though it would not be easy because of the way the plot was sited, he managed to fit in a house with the main bedroom downstairs, so, all being well, it would meet our future needs. With planning permission applied for, we looked to see if there was any statutory funding available to help build the house, but this was not to be. I therefore looked into other sources of funding and found a self-build scheme which allowed you to stay in your old home while building your new one. This sounded fine in principle, but in reality it also seemed a bit dangerous, so we decided to sell our bungalow first to fund the purchase of the plot of land.

This whole process seemed to go on forever, while the housing market was starting to turn from boom to bust. In turn there was a problem gaining planning permission due to a slight oversight by the architect. This problem was thankfully resolved with great relief as the owner of the plot of land was a member of the Freemasons and as such was able to let us know who would be able to resolve things quickly. While we had concerns that things may have to be curtailed, the owner of the plot would often ring up and say, 'What're you doing this afternoon, boy?' and if I happened to say, 'Nothing much,' I would usually be invited to tea and to watch the rugby.

While still waiting for things to happen on the planning front, a friend of mine who had recently opened a restaurant invited us there for a meal, after which my friend and his wife joined us and brought over a bottle of wine. If a wine glass is the right shape I can hold it. However, on this occasion, although I could hold the wine glass, I could not get my wheelchair under the dining room table, so every time I tried to put my glass down it appeared that I wanted more wine and was duly given some. My head was soon spinning and we had to leave early, with me in the car with an ice-cream container on my lap in case things got worse!

On another occasion we were invited to the restaurant again for my friend's baby's christening party, which was great, as I was able to see lots of old friends, some of whom I had not seen since my accident. This, though, ended up with people saying, 'Great to see you again, David,' and topping up my glass with wine or beer. While I was trying to take things easier on this occasion, I was still a bit the worse for wear, so we said our goodbyes and left slightly earlier than planned. I was still using my lightweight wheelchair at that time, which I could push a bit when it was on the level, so while my partner was opening the back of the car I decided to try and get closer to the front door to make things easier for her. As it was dark I didn't realise the car was parked on a bit of a slope, and the wheelchair started to roll down the hill. Unable to stop it, I threw myself out onto the ground, where I lay unconscious with blood pouring from a head wound.

My partner, distraught and in tears, got some people from the restaurant to check me over and I soon regained consciousness. With everyone urging me to go to the hospital to get checked over, I believe I said, 'Can we not just go home and go to bed? I should be okay by the morning.' Thankfully, common sense prevailed and I was taken to the local hospital, where some glue was put into a wound I had above my eye. Thankfully, X-rays revealed no other problems, but I stayed in overnight for observation. The next day an excruciating pain in my jaw forced me to see a dentist, who informed me that I would have to have a tooth out as I had cracked it right up to the root in the fall. I was then told that the tooth next to it was also badly cracked and would also have to come out, and in the end I was left with a big gap in my teeth.

Luckily, a few years later the senior houseman who had admitted me at Stoke Mandeville was now a consultant at Odstock spinal unit in Salisbury (now part of Salisbury District Hospital), where I would now go for treatment. I had a great rapport with him, and in conjunction with the oral surgeon at Salisbury he was able to arrange for a dental implant as it

would help with my daily activities. A few weeks after my fall from the wheelchair we thankfully got planning permission to build the house, although with the housing market still plummeting we had to drop the price on our bungalow a lot. We also had to find temporary accommodation, so we approached Social Services (now Social Care) to ask for the use of a small bungalow we knew was available at a rehabilitation centre where my partner had worked for years before becoming a hospice nurse. Strangely, the request to use the bungalow was turned down, and on inquiring why, I was told that it was due to a policy procedure being implemented by the new director of the local Social Services office. I asked for a meeting with the new director, who had moved down from up-country and seemed to be implementing policies and procedures that were most bizarre. He arrived at the bungalow accompanied by a member of staff I had known for some years, who had always been supportive. Anyway, the new broom, so to speak, tried to explain his new policies and procedures to me and my partner while the other staff member sat quietly, probably as bewildered as we were by the things being said. The new broom was then given both barrels by me and my partner. What planet was this guy on?

Despite our protestations, his decision was apparently still final. Having reflected on things overnight, the next day we contacted an acquaintance who knew our history and a visit was arranged for that afternoon. After a more reasonable discussion we were informed that the bungalow would be made available to us. Tragically, after all this, and with the sale of our property nearing completion, the man selling the plot of land passed away. This left us in complete limbo, wondering if his wife would still honour the commitment. Thankfully, having mourned her husband, she eventually agreed to abide by his decision.

Following the sale of our bungalow, we moved into the temporary accommodation while building work started on the house. Though at first overjoyed, we got letters almost weekly saying that problems with the house would mean increased costs, and while we had built in a large contingency fund, this soon evaporated, along with our proposed savings, and some of the building work had to be abandoned.

With house prices falling still further, we then had a letter from the building society saying that they would not now honour the agreed mortgage. This again had us in a complete panic until, with advice from a relative, I was able to overcome this problem and get the building society back on board. While the building work was going on, my partner would often visit the site to see how things were going and plan the interior, this being her forte. The building of the house took approximately six months, and though we had used virtually all our savings and had

to curtail much of the work, and although life would not be as easy as we had hoped, we still felt extremely proud of our achievement and our new home.

My partner continued to work as a hospice nurse while I continued to do voluntary work for various charities, although this did not include the HCBA as a new chief executive was restructuring it with it eventually becoming Hospitality Action. However, much of the voluntary work that I did still involved the hospitality industry, as I was able to accumulate various prizes and holiday breaks that could later be auctioned. One holiday in particular, back in the early '90s, raised an amazing £7,000 for the Spinal Injuries Association at one of its fundraising race days, which were held at various racecourses. Later, I was also fortunate enough, thanks to some other fundraising, to attend one of the Spinal Injuries Association's AGMs, which on this occasion was held at the superb Williams F1 Conference Centre. This was not only a great day out, as I was able to mix with others in a situation similar to my own, it also seemed somewhat unreal being so close to the F1 racing cars driven by various world champions and racing heroes of the past. The nearest I had got to seeing a live Grand Prix or racing cars of that calibre before was while playing with Scalextric as a child! I also used to do ambassador work for the Holiday Care Service and was even invited to the House of Lords some years later when the charity became Holiday Care (*now Tourism for All*). I also occasionally used to do some printing from home using the computer equipment that was, as usual, supplied by the Sequal Trust – usually through my fundraising. Though I was not earning a lot from the printing, it was always a help.

Around this time we felt drawn to the Cavalier King Charles breed of dog. I was often told that I should get a dog for company, but as I was not really independent at that time, and a big dog would have needed a great deal of exercise, it would have been unfair both on the dog and on my partner. We had previously considered getting a cat, but as the house was near a busy road there would always be the fear of the cat getting injured or worse. However, looking more into the care and needs of the Cavalier, it transpired that they only needed short walks, made superb family dogs and were great company. Having enquired about local breeders and visited one, we couldn't wait for our new family member. Some weeks later we went to choose a puppy from a litter of pups who were ready to leave their mother and came home with the puppy proudly sitting in the front seat of the car. It was not easy to house train her, but eventually things worked out and she was spoilt rotten. We tried to keep her in the kitchen at first but her whimpers soon had her in our bedroom – often on our bed – and she always gave a great deal of love and companionship.

A year or so later health and safety in relation to moving and handling people was starting to kick in with various organisations and agencies. Not long after this I asked Social Services if I could be supplied with a small item that would enable me to pick things up off the floor and was told this would require a 'visit'. It then transpired that another new broom was in place and wanted a good nose around our house! On this particular visit the person in question should have been breathing fire instead of air, as they came across as a right dragon. While I was informed that I could, in fact, have the small item, I was then informed that a portable hoist would have to be used to move me in future. I then argued that that was all very well, but where would the hoist be placed? This question was completely brushed aside as the new broom asked if they could look upstairs.

My partner and I both retorted almost simultaneously that upstairs had nothing to do with a hoist needed for someone who only used the ground floor and couldn't go upstairs! This then had the person backtracking a bit as they had realised how over-intrusive they were being. I couldn't believe the attitude of the person, and though mine is not perfect, at times I thought they were not someone I could deal with in the future, as their lack of understanding of my disability and family situation beggared belief. This visit, combined with the fact that work still needed to be done on the house to make it more suitable for our long-term future, had me seeking advice from the Spinal Injuries Association and RADAR.

I was told to ask for a review of my partner's and my needs and to start the process of a complaint against Social Services. This, despite everything I had been through since my accident, again had me totally bewildered, even though I thought I was well clued up. I therefore requested a review of our needs, which started the complaints process, which would require a further 'visit'. With the visit on this occasion involving three visitors, I thought why not also invite Uncle Tom Cobbley and all?

In a 12-page report put together by Social Services there were numerous inconsistencies and many mistruths, and how it never resulted in me being taken away by the men in white coats or worse I do not know! In time I was able to get my head around things, do some research and put together a much longer report than that produced by Social Services, highlighting all their inconsistencies and putting right all their mistruths. Thankfully, I was also able to get someone from RADAR to represent me at the complaints panel, as my partner had had enough of such things by now! The panel turned out to be a complete charade, with everyone agreeing that I had been misrepresented and that a proper assessment of need would now be put into

place. This resulted in most of the building work that had been shelved while the house was built now being agreed. Life was therefore again put on hold somewhat while the building work was undertaken.

During this time I was advised by my partner to try and look into the possibility of driving, as technology had moved on a great deal and Motability were considering funding vehicles for severely disabled drivers such as myself. I was already aware that Cornwall had a superb Mobility Centre that could help people with disabilities to drive. At that time the centre was based at an old hospital where I had stayed following an operation at Stoke Mandeville and thankfully was set in superb grounds, as the assessment vehicle seemed to have every gadget under the sun inside it. I was initially advised to try joystick steering, and as if I wasn't already concerned enough about driving again for the first time in 15 years, the joystick steering had me almost changing the colour of my underpants!

When my first test drive had me going up the grass kerb and towards a field, it was decided to try something less complex, so off I went again, trying to keep my cheeks together, and on this occasion things were a bit easier, though still daunting. Afterwards, I was informed that I had met the criteria for driving and would be put on the waiting list for funding for a 'drive from wheelchair' vehicle. This was agreed by Motability some months later. The volunteer driver who took me to the Mobility Centre on the day in question, and on numerous other occasions before that, I never saw again. Presumably he thought, 'I don't want to be anywhere near this guy if he does eventually get one of those adapted vehicles!'

While the new building work was going on there would be a period of three weeks during which I would not be able to stay at home as our downstairs bedroom and bathroom were being modified. Thankfully, it was agreed by Social Services that instead of going into residential care I could use the same amount of funding to stay elsewhere. This was during the winter, when the price of accommodation would not be so high, and I was able to stay in two self-catering cottages in Cornwall, a B&B in Devon and a further self-catering cottage in Devon. During this period I also saw an advert in *Caterer & Hotelkeeper* announcing that the Holiday Care Service, in conjunction with various other charities and hospitality industry organisations, was putting on a conference in respect of the forthcoming Disability Discrimination Act (*now part of the Equality Act*) at the Thistle Marble Arch, which was adjacent to the Churchill.

During my time at the Churchill the Thistle was a rather run-down hotel. Recently, though, it had undergone a multi-million pound refurbishment, including ten wheelchair-accessible rooms, while the Churchill had undertak-

en an even costlier refurbishment. I found the accessible rooms at the Thistle to be absolutely superb, and at the time they were probably some of the best in the country. This made life much easier for my PA/carer. The conference was superb, the various speakers including MPs and ministers, along with Lord Rix and Robert Peel, who was then the acting chief executive of Thistle Hotels. There were only a few other disabled people at the conference and, strangely, only one other wheelchair user. The morning session of the conference was of great interest and it was wonderful to see how Lord Rix and Robert Peel made the disabled people at the conference feel that their requests for more suitable facilities within the hospitality industry, even if they appeared trivial, were still important.

Robert Peel then explained that following the refurbishment of the Thistle Marble Arch, the hotel had had great returns from disabled people and organisations, and that its biggest return that year on a conference had come from an organisation associated with disabled people. During lunch, my PA/carer and I took up a table followed by two other delegates. I was asked by one of the delegates who I was and what company I was involved with. I explained that I was not involved with a company but that in my own simple way I just tried to make things easier for other disabled people within the hospitality industry where possible. 'What sort of work is that, then?' I was asked, and replied, 'One thing I try to do is to get hotels to provide wheel-in showers as opposed to baths.' Before I was able to proceed any further I was told, 'My chairman likes to soak in a bath as opposed to using a shower.' I replied, 'That may be very well and nice for your chairman, who can lead an almost independent life and can get in and out of the bath. However, while I also like to soak in the bath, people like myself are not as fortunate as your chairman. Therefore, wheel-in showers are more universally beneficial for all concerned.'

The gentleman at the table then said, 'I totally agree with what you are saying.' I looked at his name badge and it said 'Operations Director, Thistle Hotels'. I then replied, 'I'm glad about that, as your chief executive also agreed with this same philosophy when I wrote to him, and agreed that wheel-in showers in conjunction with baths would be provided wherever possible at all your hotels in the future.' I then looked at the other delegate and sort of thought *touché*! Following the conference my PA/carer and I went over to the Churchill to have a look round the new lobby, reception and restaurant areas. When one of the staff asked if we needed any assistance I explained that I used to work at the hotel and hoped it was OK to have a look round. The staff member very kindly called the general manager, who came out and met us and got the executive chef to gives us a more guided tour, so to

speak, which included the new kitchen and new pastry departments, which was all very much appreciated.

In the evening we decided to go down Park Lane and then on to Piccadilly to get a cheap meal. Ironically, on passing Grosvenor House I saw a sign advertising the *Caterer and Hotelkeeper's* Catey Awards, the hospitality industry's equivalent to the Oscars, which were being held that night. We decided to wait outside and sort of stargaze, and saw the likes of Prue Leith and Gary Rhodes enter the hotel. Both said hello, no doubt wondering who I was, as I was still in my suit. Some of the delegates from the conference earlier in the day started to come down Park Lane, followed closely behind by Liz Smith-Mills, who was a former Catey Award-winning housekeeper, and whom I had met previously at various catering exhibitions locally. All said hello and asked if I needed any help to get into the hotel – it must have looked as if I had an invitation. All I said was, 'Thanks for your very kind offer but I have a more important dinner engagement tonight!' Ironically, after the Thistle Marble Arch showed the 'business case' of making provision for disabled guests over 15 years ago, the trend with many new hotels and those undertaking refurbishments now seems to be to incorporate spa and eco-friendly facilities. While the restaurants of these hotels are usually accessible, other areas may not be so accessible or disability friendly. The proprietors of these establishments or their appointed architects or designers have therefore obviously not heard of 'inclusive design', or thought of how a loved one or other family members or friends could use such an establishment should their loved one, other family members or friends become disabled in the future. As mentioned later in this introduction, the 2012 Olympics and the Paralympics will be the biggest sporting occasions to happen in Great Britain for many years. Hopefully, being the host nation, Great Britain will have more Olympian and Paralympian medal winners than at any other Olympics. Hence, it would be great if more establishments could think of the benefits of accommodating disabled people and make greater disability provision.

When I returned home it was superb to have greater accessibility and space. This, combined with better accommodation for myself and my live-in PA/carers, would make life easier for everyone in the future. This was around the time that people were able to have control of their own care packages, so we were able to have occasional periods of respite care, and while most of the people were great, you would get the occasional person who would leave your accommodation not as they had found it! This would often result in my partner having to tidy up after other people – galling for her, especially as she was still doing some of my care and running the home while still working. While the PA/carers' costs, in conjunction

with the fees charged by the various associated agencies, were vast amounts each week, my partner was entitled only to invalid care allowance from the government when doing similar care. This meant we restricted such periods of care and, combined with other things, our relationship began to deteriorate.

During this period I continued to prepare for the arrival of my Motability vehicle and had to go for various fittings at the adaptation centre. This was a long way away, and during the first fitting the adaptation company suggested an easier set up than had been previously suggested and thankfully Motability agreed this. Also, with the vehicle less complex inside it would not only be easier for me to drive but also for others. The modifications seemed to go on forever and because of the distances involved it was suggested that I use a company closer to home. This proved beneficial in two ways. Firstly, the adaptation company pointed out some areas of concern in the way that the vehicle had been adapted. Secondly, for those fittings not done at home, travelling to the new company would be much easier. Around that time Motability had a lovely man who looked after all the drive-from-wheelchair vehicles and he would visit to see how things were going, always with the best interests of each client in mind. By now the Cornwall Mobility Centre had moved to a purpose-built building in the grounds of the local hospital. They were always very supportive and had they not been around at the time, I would probably not have taken up driving. On one occasion, while at the Mobility Centre I mentioned to someone from Motability that I had not been supplied with a fire extinguisher as mentioned on my original list of recommendations. I was informed that these could be obtained from the likes of Halfords, to which I replied, 'While I am driving I am using both hands, but while I can drive the car I do not think I would be able to operate an ordinary fire extinguisher.'

About a week later I had a letter saying Motability would be putting in a fire trace system in my vehicle and in all other drive-from-wheelchair vehicles. This would prove a blessing in disguise, as a few months later I had a letter from the original adaptation company saying that a customer with a vehicle similar to mine had had problems with their fuel pipes, and that I should return my vehicle to have it checked over. As this was not practical, it was agreed that the vehicle would be checked at my own home. When the inspector arrived he briefly looked under the vehicle and pronounced everything fine, which did not seem a very comprehensive inspection. I decided to get the RAC to look over the vehicle and was informed that it was a 'potential coffin on wheels'. I knew I wanted to be cremated, but not this early in life! I therefore contacted Motability, who arranged for the original converter to rectify the problem.

For my partner, though, who was already concerned about driving the vehicle due to some of its earlier problems, this latest setback made up her mind about not driving it! Once the rectification work was done, it was therefore down to me to get on with the driving myself. This I did, with some support from Cornwall Mobility Centre and from various people who would go out with me in case I needed assistance. I would drive down to Truro and practise parking, etc., with bollards in an empty car park and, though there still needed to be some minor modifications, once I was aware of all the quirks of the new technology, I had more confidence in the vehicle and my driving became better. However, it took a backwards step when the vehicle encountered a gearbox problem and the RAC had to be called. A local recovery firm then arrived and the driver of the recovery vehicle took one look and said, 'It's a brave man who drives this!' Having looked further into the problem, he jacked up the vehicle and put it into drive with the handbrake on, as it would have to be driven back in drive. The person who was with me decided it would be best if they drove me home. The passenger seat on the vehicle was therefore put into the drive-from-wheelchair position with me in the back of the vehicle waiting to go into passenger-seat position.

While this was going on the recovery man got out his paperwork, sat on the front driver's seat and, passing me the paperwork to sign, leant on the push/pull brake/accelerator, thinking it was an arm-rest! As the vehicle was a 3.3 litre Chrysler Voyager, even with the hand-brake on we almost went into orbit before hitting the recovery man's brand new pick-up truck. Thankfully, the car park where we were was empty so nobody was hurt. When I arrived home this latest dis-aster, together with everything else that had gone on, seemed to be another nail in the coffin of my relationship with my partner! Luckily, the damage to my vehi-cle was not too great and none of the adaptations were affected, so it was returned within a few weeks. When I did get it back it was great to get out and about again and get used to driving, and though my driving was fine I felt I needed someone with me in the vehicle, so out-ings were often restricted. I did continue using my manual chair to keep my mus-cles built up as opposed to the electric wheelchair which, in conjunction with my vehicle, would give me greater independ-ence.

I was sitting at home one day in my electric wheelchair thinking how crazy it was so I decided to go out on my own. From then on, unless I needed to drive a long distance, I felt able to go out on my own, and some years later even had an endorsement from a Boeing 747 pilot, who said my driving was amazing consid-ering my limitations, and I was even asked to promote the RAC's Driving Still*Able* campaign. This new-found freedom was

Promoting the RAC's 'Driving StillAble' campaign.

great and came at just the right time – my partner had met someone else, so when I did get out of the house it was a relief. Though I had never wanted to go on a group holiday and was never really keen on cold-weather pursuits, I was encour-aged to try and get away for a while and put my name down for a Back Up course skiing in Åre, Sweden, only to find out that the trip was already fully booked. A week or so later I had a phone call to say that someone had dropped out and there was a place for me should I want it. Still somewhat daunted by the idea, I was fur-ther encouraged to go. I bought such equipment as would not be supplied by Back Up, much of it on my credit card, and then found out that maintenance work would prevent me getting to Heathrow by rail. I therefore had to bite the bullet even further and fly to Heathrow alone on a British Airways flight – and this was before the era of cheap flights! I then asked where we would stay the night and was told that accommodation had been arranged at a Marriott hotel – not exactly cheap. I decided to give the man who had arranged this a call and, lo and behold, found out that I had been in Stoke Mandeville with him 15 years or so before. I told him I would be staying at a Travel Inn, along with several others. On arriving at Heathrow I was picked up by two of the course instructors and taken to the Travel Inn, where I met most of the others on the course. My friend and I seemed to be the two old codgers on the trip! Asked then to sign a disclaimer form by one of the course instructors, I thought, 'I know I'm a bit accident prone, but what on earth will the week ahead entail?'

It was wonderful how the nurses, carers and buddies rallied round to get everyone on the flight to Sweden and then transferred to another flight followed by a further transfer onto a bus which would take us to our hotel. After a good night's sleep we were all up early to start our first day's skiing. It took about an hour to put on layers of thermals, coats, etc., before venturing out into the extreme cold, but in many respects it did not feel cold. However, this did not stop a sort of dodgem-car race during the lunch break every day to be the first to get to the log fire in the restaurant. The skiing was absolutely superb, although difficult during the first few days while the ski karts were adapted to each person's

Skiing down a mountain in Åre, Sweden.

individual needs.

At the end of each day's skiing we would have a 'team briefing', which my friend and I, while realising the benefit of it, often found amusing, as it felt like being back at school. One evening we were informed that we would have 'the opportunity of a lifetime' to watch the women's leg of the world championship downhill skiing, which was being held that night in Åre. It was thought we should all go, but nobody *had* to go, and we were asked if any of us didn't want to go, to which my friend replied, 'I don't want to go,' followed by me timidly saying, 'I also don't want to go,' as we both wanted to stay in and keep warm after being out skiing all day. This attitude didn't go down too well with 'team bonding' and it was felt that someone should stay behind to help us, so after further discussion we said that if we were sorted out before they went we would be alright on our own.

When everyone had left we took our places by the lovely warm log fire and asked the barmaid to get us a couple of beers and put Sky Sports on. Ironically, the women's downhill event was being shown on Sky, and we were nice and warm by the fire drinking lager while the temperature on the TV screen stated it was -22 degrees outside! When everyone eventually returned we asked if they had had a good time and most appeared to say 'Yes' through clenched teeth while rigor mortis seemed to be setting in!

The next day, being our penultimate day, was spent undertaking various tests to see what sort of ski licence we would get, although we weren't told this. This was followed by an afternoon of free skiing, and during the evening we were informed what sort of ski licence we would be given. The awards ceremony was great fun and gave a sense of great personal achievement to many. I was given a blue licence, which meant I could ski independently with others in the future if I wished. After spending almost 15 years moving at approximately 4mph it seemed amazing that during the week I had been told off for going too fast and for trying to attempt small ski jumps with the kart. In hindsight, maybe I should have gone on this kind of course earlier!

On returning home I felt totally shattered but had greater confidence about doing similar things in the future. To help repay Back Up for the opportunity of going on the holiday I suggested that they apply for funding to the Trusthouse Charitable Foundation, which at that time was able to help various charities. Ironically, though I had been working for Trusthouse Forte hotels (later re-formed as the Rocco Forte Collection) at the time of my accident, and in many respects had been badly let down by the hotel where I was working at the time, when I did receive support from various sources the Trusthouse Charitable Foundation would usually match any support or help given. At one stage I was also awarded a bursary by the Lord Forte Foundation to undertake some access work which was due to be given by Lord Forte himself, along with other members of the Forte family. As this was at the time of the hostile takeover of Trusthouse Forte by Granada, the meeting never happened, although I was still given the bursary and in turn undertook an access course via the Centre for Accessible Environments. After the holiday I looked into sources of care different from those I had used previously and found that most of the people were foreign. While this was strange at first, some of these people were superb while occasionally some would come for the wrong reasons, which could cause problems.

During the next year or so I went gliding on several occasions, all fantastic experiences, and though I was not really able to control the glider fully I was able to fly it almost semi-solo at times. Similarly, I was encouraged to abseil down a local fire station tower to raise funds for the Cornwall Blind Association. While this, in principle, seemed a good

Gliding from Perranporth Airport.

opportunity, when one of the Marines organising the event tried to give me a fireman's lift up the ladder of the tower I started to slip out of his grip! It was then decided to use an abseiling technique to get me up the inside of the tower before the big descent down the outside. I had my eyes tightly closed until some rather strong language from the Marine abseiling down the tower with me, who said, 'You've paid your money, so open your beeping eyes!' I duly obliged! Though everyone else attending gave me a good round of applause, I was in absolute agony for the next two weeks and decided to curtail such activities in future. However, I got a phone call from Back Up a few years later, having raised further funds for the charity, and was offered another ski course in Åre to see if I could get a red licence or bi-ski. While the offer of this course was a great gesture and the week was amazing in many respects,

due to being older and because my energy levels were much lower since my accident, I was demoted, so to speak, in the licence department! I therefore felt that this should be the end of such vigorous adventures.

Later on, the Occupational Therapy department at the local hospital thankfully helped make up a fishing splint for me and I was able to go fishing a few times. This usually involved catching small carp at a few pools near Newquay with a friend, and oh, to have or find a wheelchair accessible boat locally to go sea fishing again! Likewise, to go big game fishing or scuba diving in warm waters, as these were two things that were on my wish list while in Bermuda before my accident curtailed things! The fishing sessions were always great, as sometimes they would be followed by a barbecue at my friend's house. On one such occasion I asked my friend to put some wood on the barbecue as the sun had moved and I was starting to get a bit cold. Some minutes later a hot splinter flew out of the

Fishing at Mawgan Porth Pools.

barbecue and landed on my jumper, which started to catch fire and had me flapping around furiously trying to put it out. I knew I always wanted to be known as 'hot', so to speak, but not that hot! Luckily my friend was close by to stop me going completely up in smoke, and from then on I was nicknamed 'Guy'! Earlier, I had applied for lottery funding which enabled me to set up a website highlighting various accessible restaurants, hotels, B&Bs, self-catering accommodation and other holiday provision throughout the South West, parts of Scotland and London. Likewise, I was able to expand the website project further thanks in part to a grant from the Savoy Educational Trust. While in London on one occasion I was fortunate, with part of my funding, to be able to stay at the Chelsea Village Hotel *(now Millennium & Copthorne Hotels at Chelsea Football Club)*, and I even managed to get tickets to see Chelsea play Wimbledon while both teams were still in the top flight. Though the old Shed End and North Stand had been completed, the new stadium was still not fully completed but it was still almost full so it would be great to return on another occasion. How things have changed, though, as I recall watching Chelsea at home in the '70s when I was working in London where the crowds at times would be only 7,000–8,000. It is almost impossible to get tickets now, as I found out on a recent visit to London. In turn, the catering facil-

ities and outlets now run by the Compass Group run into millions of pounds a year and provide superb food compared to the greasy burgers that were generally all that was available when watching Chelsea in the '70s. Though I had already completed a website course at a local college, I was only able to create a basic website, so a postgraduate student who worked for a company run by a relative designed the website using my suggestions for the layout and did a superb job. With my new Motability vehicle I was then out and about all over Devon and Cornwall taking photographs of various establishments for the website and writing reviews. The vehicle also enabled me to get to see various karate tournaments locally, and although these were not as competitive as in my day due to various political and other splits within the karate world, it was still good to see how people I had once trained or trained with had progressed. While attending such events I would always be more in tune with the Kumite (sparring) than the Kata (form), as the

Driving thanks to a vehicle from Motability

style of karate I had done previously had changed many of its Katas. Combined with the fact that when I was training in London for two years it was with different organisations performing different Katas, this meant I concentrated mostly on Kumite. For those who do not know much about karate, or about my time doing it, I initially started, as mentioned previously, in my local village hall. I was 14 at the time and the youngest of those who joined. A yellow belt and a purple belt taught us – we thought for some time that the latter was a black belt, as the colour of his belt was so dark! Most of the time we thought they were superb, as they could run rings round us. The purple belt was a colossal man compared to me and very kindly would sometimes take me to other training sessions in his car. Unfortunately, though, he had to restrict his karate in the summer as he owned and ran a surf shop, café and car park at a beach not far from my home. We therefore spent a lot of time being taught by the yellow belt, but the training was still good. When some people were sparring they would go a bit overboard and there would be slight injuries. Similarly, we would have a club competition occasionally and afterwards most people would have bruised bodies, bleeding lips and noses and the occasional loose tooth. This seemed to be par for the course back then, and thankfully I was not often on the receiving end of things! We also used to have training sessions once a

Practising karate while on a summer course.

month with Jim Cooper, who would travel from Redruth. Jim was 18 at the time, I believe, and the youngest Dan grade (black belt) in Britain. He and his elder brother Dave, another Dan grade, ran the Redruth Dojo (place of the way). Great people and superb at karate, they would later become England internationals.

Our club was part of the British Karate Association, and I later gained my Dan grade (black belt) under the BKA, which at that time included some of the first Japanese karate exponents to come to Britain and for us consisted mainly of Wado-Ryu karate. The members of my grading panel were Peter Spanton, Ticky Donovan, Toru Takamizawa and John Smith. I was also fortunate that early in my training I went on one of the last summer courses held by the BKA in Hayle,

Cornwall. The week was absolutely fantastic and was attended by over 300 people as well as some of the best karate exponents in Britain, including Ticky Donovan who, a year later as a member of the British team, won the world championships, beating Japan in the finals – a remarkable achievement at the time. John Smith, our main Sensei (instructor) within the BKA, was a formidable exponent at Kumite and Kata, having been a British team and individual champion in both. He would come to Redruth to do training sessions and we would go to Plymouth for training sessions while others would have gradings. Most of my early gradings, though, were done under Dave and Jim Cooper in Redruth, and as I was young, and supple I rose through the grades quickly, even being double graded on one occasion. This led to a rather awkward situation; on the same day as my double grading, our purple belt club instructor went for his brown belt, which, because his work commitments meant he was unable to train regularly, he unfortunately failed to get. This put me six months ahead of everyone else at the club and on the same grade as the club instructor! At the end of our next training session we finished with a bit of a competition and, ironically, I ended up having to fight my now co instructor. As I was only 15 and he was almost twice my body weight and age, I tried to use my agility to the maximum during the fight and placed a superb Jodan Mawashi Geri (roundhouse

kick to the head) which rocked my opponent's head but was perfectly controlled and deemed an Ippon (one full point or decisive blow) by the student who was judging, and in turn it won me the fight. This made my opponent none too happy and left everyone else wondering what might happen next. Luckily, things got taken in good faith so it was not my turn on this occasion for a bit of excessive contact! John Smith had earlier set up the Bujinkai Karate Association using his own style and as a club we became part of it. Bujinkai was a combination of Wado-Ryu karate and Praying Mantis kung fu, much of it influenced by Danny Connor. Danny, also high up in the BKA, had learnt Praying Mantis kung fu and I and others would go to various training sessions held by him in conjunction with John Smith in Plymouth. I also went on another summer course in Cornwall, many of the sessions being held by Danny Connor and including superb weapons training.

Ticky Donovan also set up his own style, calling it Ishinryu. The Bujinkai instructor and students were extremely competitive in every contest they entered. I was fortunate enough later on to fight in one of their teams in the British championships at Crystal Palace, where Bujinkai were denied the chance of a team medal after meeting Ishinryu in the quarter finals. However, on other occasions they would be more successful, with individual medals won by various members of the squad, some of who made it into the

England and British teams. Earlier, I was also lucky enough, thanks to friends, to attend a course in London under the legendary Dominic Valera, and also to see Dave and Jim Cooper both become British full contact karate champions at the first event of its kind to be held in Britain at Belle Vue, Manchester. Likewise, I was able to see a superb Kyokushinkai knockdown karate competition in London attended by Steve Arneil and the legendary Mas Oyama. I was also fortunate, as mentioned previously, in that I was able to train more freely while working in London. Most of these training sessions would be with Ticky Donovan at his Dojo (place of the way) in Dagenham and at Tyrone Whyte's Dojo. Ticky Donovan was three times British karate champion in the 1970s and, after deciding to no longer contest the championship, his student, Tyrone Whyte, became British champion.

While training at Tyrone's Dojo one evening we had a club competition against Dicky Wu and Mike Dinsdale's students. While learning karate you were taught to show a great deal of respect for your senior grades, that you should usually be well attired and show respect to others and that there should be only light contact to the head. However, there would be times when someone ignored all this. During this competition, when my opponent stood up, he had virtually no sleeve on one arm of his Gi (karate suit). He didn't bow to me or to the referee as expected, the referee on this occasion

being Tyrone Whyte. I wondered what the fight might entail and after a while landed a chudan-suki (body punch) on my opponent while he landed a Jodan Mawashi Geri (roundhouse kick to the head) on me. With both of us scoring points at the same time no one was given a point. However, my opponent had not controlled his kick, and I dropped to the floor with a ringing noise in my ear. Tyrone then checked me over to see if I was OK. At first all appeared well and I was awarded the fight as my opponent had used excessive contact – not an acceptable way to fight – which also left me feeling unable to fight any further that evening due to feeling not quite right. The next day, while scratching my ear I noticed blood on my finger and was diagnosed with a perforated eardrum at St Thomas's Hospital. This injury by default, so to speak, was thankfully my only real injury while doing karate.

While doing karate you were also taught to use your skills only in the defence of yourself or your family and friends, in the instance of extreme danger or unprovoked attack, or in the support of law and order. This only happened to me on three occasions, one of which was while I was working for the Savoy Group at Stone's Chop House in Piccadilly. I was taking a break from work with others outside and watching the football results that were displayed on a revolving noticeboard on the Swiss Centre. Suddenly, a police car with its siren wailing came zooming round Piccadilly followed by another police car doing the same. A man then came running towards the alleyway where we were standing followed by someone behind shouting, 'Stop him, stop him!' Possibly not thinking sensibly, I landed a reverse punch directly into the man's face. This stopped him in his tracks, and his pursuer grabbed him from behind. When I followed up the punch with a roundhouse kick to the head, the man I had kicked rebounded into the other man, whose head hit a wall and both men dropped to the ground. Wondering what on earth I'd done, I got in the restaurant lift and stopped it between floors while the other chefs were shouting, 'David, where are you? The police want to see you!' I thought to myself 'I'm going nowhere!' – I could have just taken out two members of the Mafia for all I knew!

After a while I emerged to be told that, thankfully, no one was seriously injured. The police came to see me a few days later to thank me, although one policeman still had a sore head, as he was the one who had grabbed the man from behind. I was informed by the police that the man I had hit had stolen a lot of jewellery from a jewellers, so his proposed charges of assault, grievous bodily harm and attempted murder by me would thankfully not stand up in court!

Another bizarre but funny thing happened while I was working at the Savoy. This was in 1977, the year of the Queen's silver jubilee and the year that Virginia Wade won the ladies' singles event at Wimbledon. While leaving the Savoy I started to cross the road to go to the tube station and saw some sports stars coming out of the banqueting suite at the front of the Savoy. Thinking there must have been a sports award lunch going on I decided to stargaze for a while and saw various people coming out of the hotel, including Virginia Wade and, shortly afterwards, Ticky Donovan wearing his Great Britain karate team jacket. I then thought, 'Blimey, I'd better bow to him or I could be in for some extra knuckle press ups at my next training session.' Afterwards, I thought Ticky probably never saw me, and with my work colleagues coming across the road they must have thought I was a right prat bowing while in turn appearing to pay homage to the Savoy!

Ishinryu, along with many of their students, usually made up the backbone of the British, European and future World team squads, so my training sessions with Ishinryu were superb. Ticky Donovan was the England team coach and, as mentioned previously, had I not gone to Bermuda to work I would possibly have made it into the England under-21 squad. Later, under Ticky's guidance and coaching, England would become one of the most successful karate countries in the world. Likewise, two individuals, one being Vic Charles, whom I trained with at Ishinryu while working in London, along with Wayne Otto, who unfortunately I never saw compete, became the most successful Kumite fighters ever under WKF *(the Olympic recognised Federation)* rules, and whose records remain unsurpassed to this day. After my accident I had been with friends to the British championships in Birmingham. Such support was great but could not always be relied on due to other people's commitments. It was suggested to me by John Smith that I keep going to local tournaments and training sessions so that I could continue up the grades and train people from my wheelchair, but this was not possible at that time due to my circumstances and living arrangements – and I was not independent then.

The disciplines of karate and of being a chef have moved on so much over the last 30 years that they remain somewhat distant memories to me – or possibly these are just senior moments! It would be great to still be involved in karate or the hospitality industry, but I feel the complications associated with my spinal injury and life in general preclude this so I'm happy to take an armchair view of things, so to speak. Plus, following my accident, my energy levels were never that high. With aging these have decreased further, so I am happy to combine some limited work with voluntary work while sometimes being on the receiving end of good fortune from others. You will, though, see how some people featured in the Dinner Party section

of this book are able to combine incredible careers and pastimes while being tetraplegic. I did write to Jimmy Saville twice at Stoke Mandeville a few years after my accident to see if I could attend the world karate championships when he was doing the TV programme 'Jim'll Fix It', but Jim didn't 'Fix It' for me! While huge numbers of people participate in karate worldwide, and though it was, I believe, initially shortlisted, along with squash, for the 2012 Olympics, two other sports having been dropped, the IOC members, in their wisdom, decided not to vote for karate to be included, so the 2012 games remain two sports down.

Karate was again shortlisted for the 2016 Olympics but missed out, strangely, to golf and rugby sevens, neither of which is exactly participated in worldwide or involves the number of people who take part in karate. Similarly, while golf and rugby sevens either need lush areas of grass or large open spaces in which to practise and participate, karate can be practised and participated in anywhere in the world using only a small hall or outdoor area. Likewise, karate can be participated in by people from varying backgrounds, as opposed to golf, which could be deemed an elite sport. The World Karate Federation has now included a disability karate section in their championships, as has the British Karate Federation. We will be the host nation in 2012 – wouldn't it be great if karate could be included somewhere within the

At the Eden Project with a nurse from my time in ICU in Bermuda.

2012 Olympics or Paralympics so it could be showcased to the world? If not, it would be hoped that the IOC includes karate in the 2020 Olympics as it has been shortlisted for possible inclusion. Karate has many more participants around the world than the other sports under consideration!

As well as attending local karate tournaments, my new vehicle meant I was also able to see more of Cornwall and attend many of the concerts at the Eden Project, as well as take various carers sightseeing along with a nurse who had cared for me while working in the ICU in Bermuda, who had travelled all the way from America for a holiday.

Back to my website! Once launched, it proved to be quite ground-breaking, and the communications manager of one of the largest hotel chains in the country

called it one of the best on the internet. Similarly, a consultant from Holiday Care *(now Tourism for All)* felt the website was the way forward in showing what various establishments were like. Around this time one of my friends from years back got in contact and told me about a reunion he was organising. This was another blessing in disguise, as a live-in carer who was giving support at the time informed us that there was a problem with the shower unit in her room and could I have a look. It turned out that the shower had been leaking for over a week, which had caused a lot of damage! This, combined with everything else that had gone on in the past, resulted in my partner deciding to move out of the house and me thinking I might need to sell it as part of a settlement. Thankfully, though, I was able to find a temporary solution to this problem some time later. The reunion therefore came at a very apt time and it was great to meet up with people I had not seen for years, many of whom had not seen me in a wheelchair. Following the reunion I was encouraged to drive to Plymouth and meet up with friends to see Argyle play on a regular basis. While doing the website I also went to see Cornwall play in the rugby county championships and they managed to make it into the semi-finals. The game was to be played away against Yorkshire and as my funding included looking at various hotels and self-catering apartments in Yorkshire, I was able to watch Cornwall make it into the county championship final to be played at Twickenham. Fortunately, one of the local radio stations arranged a train to London, and with everyone dressed in black and gold, with painted faces, others eating pasties and drinking beer and cider, etc. and cracking jokes it made for a superb journey.

The friend who had contacted me earlier regarding the reunion – jokingly known as our 'Leader', as most things he arranged involved humour – was supposed to have made arrangements for everyone to meet up in a pub, but, as usual, things went a bit pear-shaped as the pub was about two miles from Twickenham – too far for my friends to push me. Everyone therefore came to the stadium, where our 'Leader' arranged for everyone to drink in one of the bars. The bar we found could only be accessed via steps, so as I was in my lightweight wheelchair, two of the people with me, and sober, lifted me up the steps. You could hardly move in the bar, with everyone wanting a drink and then badgering our 'Leader', as it was now his round. While I was speaking to friends my wheelchair was grabbed by our 'Leader' and we all wondered what on earth was going to happen next. He started to push me towards the bar shouting, 'Man in a wheelchair wants a drink!' It was like the parting of the Red Sea, with everyone in hysterics! After a few more drinks everyone took up their various places in the

stadium and it was great to see Cornwall win the county championship, with most of *Trelawney's Army* joining the team on the pitch to celebrate.

On returning home everyone reflected on the fantastic day out, which would probably never be repeated. I did continue to watch rugby occasionally in Cornwall as one of my friend's sons would end up becoming one of the Cornish Pirates' longest serving players before moving to Wales to play for teams in the Magners League. I was later fortunate enough to watch the Pirates win the British and Irish Cup. It would therefore be great if a Stadium for Cornwall could be realised, thus enabling the Pirates to play in the Premiership along with bringing top class rugby to the county. Following the trip to Twickenham I completed the website project and then saw a leaflet in Asda asking, 'Could you change your life with £10,000?' This intrigued me, so I filled in a simple form stating various aspects of life planning and was then shortlisted to fill in a further form and shortlisted again for an interview. On the form I had been asked to fill in my further goals, which at the time were to take a holiday to Florida followed by a P&O cruise and then to write a book about making life easier for disabled people travelling. The funding would be coming from City & Guilds under their *Future 100* promotion and would enable 100 people from around the world to take a City & Guilds course to fulfil their goals. My interview went really well and a few days later I had a phone call to say that I had been successful and would be one of the City & Guilds *Future 100* bursary winners. When asked to give details of the funding I required, in my haste I included the cost of a cruise and

At the Millennium Dome with other Future 100 *award winners.*

a holiday in Florida, together with the funding needed to take a City & Guilds course. When, a few days later, I was informed that a holiday to Florida and a cruise were not deemed part of a City & Guilds course, I had to accept that you win a few and lose a few! If I had got things right in the first place I would have had fantastic support and been extremely well trained.

The *Future 100* awards ceremony was held at the Millennium Dome (*now O2 Arena*), which at that time was open with all the exhibitions in place. It was great to be able to see around the Dome and to meet all the other *Future 100* bursary winners. The ceremony was extremely humbling, as some of the other winners came from very impoverished countries and backgrounds. I undertook the course that I had been given funding for and

then looked to take on further work, and got a job with Disability Cornwall updating their website. With this work and my own website project completed, I began to attend Hotelympia to do some fundraising and would often see members of Hospitality Action, along with the then editor of *Caterer & Hotelkeeper*.

The ironic thing about my visit to the Millennium Dome was that earlier in the year the late Christopher Reeve, the former Superman actor, had also visited London with his family to highlight the need for funding to find a cure for the devastating effects of spinal injuries, and the family had visited the Dome and had a great day out. However, while this visit got a lot of publicity in many major newspapers, I understand that Christopher Reeve, while staying at one of the best hotels in London, apparently had to be lifted up the stairs of the hotel to access it along with other areas. I also recall a conversation once in which someone mentioned that going on holiday with someone with a high lesion spinal injury was like preparing for the D Day landings! This can sometimes be the case for me, as currently there are only three hotels in London with overhead hoists and only one with what I would consider a suitable shower chair combined with an overhead hoist. In a similar vein, it was great to see on television last year the programme about the £220 million refurbishment of the Savoy (a Fairmont managed hotel), where lavish amounts of money were spent on the likes of mirrors, paintings, fountains, etc. I was very fortunate indeed to stay a night at the Savoy on a complimentary basis while working at the hotel in the 1970s, when staff were put up overnight in order to be there early on Christmas Day. It would be great to stay at the Savoy now, but even if I could afford to do so it would quite impracticable, as, although the refurbished hotel now provides some wheelchair-accessible rooms with wheel-in showers, I was informed, on making an inquiry on behalf of a friend from abroad a few months after the opening, that a hoist was not available. Likewise, a shower chair was not available. Please, Mr or Mrs Hospitality Provider, please try and provide such equipment in the future or have it available for use. With the right input it need not detract from the ambiance of your establishment. Likewise, as mentioned previously, you could increase your revenue streams by providing specialised equipment and other facilities. The visually and hearing impaired, along with those with other disabilities, would, I'm sure, rather have things that meet their specific needs than the likes of a trouser press or a shoe-shine service.

Around this time, Regain – the Trust for Sports Tetraplegics was becoming more established and I started to do some fundraising for them, which led to them and others donating various hotel breaks for auction. Regain also put on an annual luncheon in London for other sports tetraplegics, organised by Action for Charity, and when I was able to attend, it was usually thanks to the Copthorne Tara Hotel – the only hotel in London at that time with an overhead hoist in one of their wheelchair-accessible rooms. The luncheons were always fantastic. I usually attended them with my sister, and it was great to meet others in a situation similar to mine and gain inspiration from their amazing achievements.

A year or so later, while visiting Hotelympia, I met the new chief executive of Hospitality Action who, along with the then editor of *Caterer & Hotelkeeper*, made me extremely welcome. The chief executive later came to my home and I was offered a small job with Hospitality Action drumming up further support for the charity. This I did in various ways and as usual was given various hotel breaks to be auctioned off, some of them so amazing they would be used at Hospitality Action's annual ball at Grosvenor House, to which I was also given an invitation. Having never attended such an event, it was great to see how the charity raised funds on such occasions. At my table were members of the Ark Foundation, which is the drug and alcohol awareness campaigning arm of Hospitality Action, and as most were working and not drinking, there were several spare half bottles of wine. With all the extra drink to tempt us, my friend and I had started to get rather pickled when, lo and behold, the chief executive of Hospitality Action asked me to announce how much had been raised during the evening and I had to try an instant detox with water! This turned out to be a rather bizarre moment – me in my wheelchair giving a speech from the dancefloor of the Great Room at Grosvenor House – like something you would see on an awards ceremony on television. It was also a great feeling to get a round of applause for explaining how Hospitality Action had contributed to my achieving a quality of life I could never have imagined following my accident.

Knowing the Ark Foundation held lectures around the country I asked to be told when they would be coming to Cornwall and a few weeks later heard that there would be a lecture at St Austell College. Peter Kay, whom I had never met, gave an amazing lecture in which he talked about his life, which in many respects mirrored my own, especially my childhood and my time in the hospitality industry. The main difference between Peter and myself was that while my career in the industry had been curtailed as a result of the diving accident in which I nearly died, Peter's time in the industry had been cut short through drug and alcohol abuse and he had also been near death. The students were fascinated by the way Peter explained the dangers of drug and alcohol abuse and how, in the hospitality industry, it was easy to become addicted due to the pressures of work and the ready availability of alcohol. He also mentioned that he was chief executive of Tony Adams's Sporting Chance Clinic.

Not long after the lecture, during a phone call from the secretary to the chief executive of Hospitality Action, I was completely nonplussed to hear that I had been nominated for an award and asked could I make it to Birmingham the following week? So a friend, a PA/carer and I made our way to Birmingham. Still not knowing what to expect I got all suited and booted and went to the hotel to meet others from Hospitality Action. On the way to the bar I again saw Liz Smith-Mills, who said, 'David what are you doing here?' to which I replied, 'I'm not really sure!' At the bar I was met by the chief executive of Hospitality Action and saw Peter Kay and Michael Quinn, both drinking Coke. I knew that Michael, the first ever British chef at The Ritz, had also lost his way in life due to alcohol abuse and that he also lectured for the Ark Foundation. I was then asked by the chief executive of Hospitality Action if I wanted a drink and thought to myself, 'How do I handle this one?' I replied, 'It's a bit early, isn't it!?'

The chief executive said that it was not too early for him and he was having a pint of Guinness, so I replied, 'Great! A pint of lager, please!' Following the drink, we all went over to the Symphony Hall, where the MARCHE (Midlands Association for Restaurants, Hotels and Entertainment) awards evening was being held. Still not sure of what was ahead, I then met other members of the Ark Foundation and we took our places at a table in a huge banqueting hall within the Symphony Hall.

It seemed that the evening would consist of various awards – young chef of the year, waiter of the year, housekeeper of the year, etc. – three people being nominated for each award and the winner receiving a bottle of champagne, a commemorative plate and a cheque for £200. My friend then said that I was probably down for an award, but I still couldn't understand what my connection with the Ark Foundation could be. I liked a few drinks occasionally so I just assumed I was asked along to make up the numbers. Shortly afterwards I was informed by the chief executive of Hospitality Action, the chairman of the Ark Foundation and the editor of *Caterer & Hotelkeeper* that I would, in fact, be getting an award. Still not sure why, I was then informed by the editor of *Caterer & Hotelkeeper* that he would be giving a short speech about the award, which I learned was to be for *Overcoming Adversity*.

The speech he gave was extremely gracious and was followed by the presentation of my bottle of champagne, commemorative plate and a cheque for £200. The chief executive of Hospitality Action advised me to put the money into a trust fund account (*David Croft*

At the MARCHE Awards with the Chief Executive of Hospitality Action, the Chairman of MARCHE, the Chairman of the Ark Foundation and the editor of Caterer & Hotelkeeper.

Celebrating the promotion of Plymouth Argyle with other members of the 'Green Army'.

Trust Fund) which he knew had been set up some years before and which usually remained dormant. On my return home everyone was intrigued as to what the award was about and said I should contact the local press about it. I decided not to, as people could have assumed I was drunk when I had my accident (a not uncommon factor in such cases), plus before writing this book I always liked to go about my life somewhat quietly.

An article did appear in Hospitality Action's newsletter and there was a piece in a Plymouth Argyle programme, one of the team managers having used the services of Sporting Chance for a player who had had various problems. The game in question was against QPR, a superb day out as Argyle secured its second promotion in a row, this time from the old Division 2 to the Championship. The following week, like many other members of the *Green Army*, I spent preparing for the final game of the season, which would see Argyle receive the championship trophy. The celebrations were superb, and coming away from that game I felt perfectly contented but with a rather sore head – not from drinking too much, but from all the beach balls and other inflatables, including some of my own, batted round the Devonport End before, during and after the game!

The future for Plymouth Argyle and the *Green Army* around this time seemed to have everyone buoyed up as the club moved further up the Championship. In turn it had been operating a healthy profit year on year and was recognised as one of the most financially stable and best-run clubs in England. Later I was fortunate enough to attend a corporate do at Home Park when a friend's wife won a corporate day out at Argyle at a charity event courtesy of 3663. The chosen game was against Hull City and had Argyle won this game they would have been within reach of a play-off place to the Premier League. Luckily, on this occasion someone was able to drive my car to the game and, as everything was on a complimentary basis thanks to 3663, the beer was flowing freely in our corporate box. Unfortunately, the football on the pitch was not flowing so freely and the game seemed destined to be a goalless draw. Hull then made a vital substitution and with five minutes to go scored a goal which would eventually see them move

With Ian Holloway at Plymouth Argyle's supporters' meeting.

above Argyle in the Championship and go on to reach the Premier League. Plymouth then became the biggest city in Europe not to reach the highest league in their respective country. This game also began the gradual decline in the fortunes of Plymouth Argyle for numerous reasons over the next few seasons bar a few highlights. This, combined with Argyle being relegated from the Championship and England failing to get the 2018 World Cup with Plymouth as a possible host city, would mean that the supposed and often alluded to golden egg, along with its many associated benefits, would never be laid! A complete meltdown of everything associated with Plymouth Argyle would soon follow; how these circumstances came about remain a mystery to many. Further misery was to follow when Argyle went into administration and were docked 10 points for being unable to meet their financial commitments. An unprecedented second relegation would follow, along with an uncertain future for the club. What that future holds nobody knows, but if Argyle are to resurrect any of their former glory, it would now seem unlikely, in my lifetime, that this will result in them reaching the so-called promised land of the Premier League! Hence, my support of the *Green Army* can sometimes now hold bittersweet memories. The ironic thing about the earlier game against QPR was that Ian Holloway, their manager at that time, would later become Plymouth Argyle's manager. Previous to this, on behalf of the Ark Foundation he had given a lecture to a group of chefs comparing the dangers of alcohol in the lives of football players and chefs, and he would also go on to assist with fundraising in connection with Sporting Chance Clinic. I got to meet Ian at a Plymouth Argyle Cornish supporters' branch meeting, together with some of the players who at that time made up the great squad at Argyle. During the season following this meeting I continued to go to games but was unable to drive myself every time as the adapted vehicle supplied by Motability was now over 10 years old and rather unreliable. I applied to Motability for a replacement and after some months was informed that my grant application was again successful and I was on the waiting list for a new vehicle. Until it arrived I tried to re-enter the hospitality industry working from home and had everything in place to welcome my first customer. I made sure that the various government departments approved everything I was doing beforehand, and though my work would not be affected, I had an extraordinary letter from one department saying that I would now require a 'visit'. This, along with other things going on at the time, and some childhood problems having resurfaced again, which could not be talked to others and were only ever known to my ex partner at the time, had me in complete personal meltdown and in turn saw me completely lose the plot to life and nearly put me in an early grave!

Thankfully, others were around to pick up the pieces and though I was once again on the brink and fighting for my life, I came through everything but was still rather fragile emotionally. Whilst it was suggested by those closest to me that I needed counselling, I was informed by the powers that be that this was not really considered appropriate at that time, but that I would be put on a waiting list and contacted at a later date. This never materialised!

Though my problems were not of the usual type associated with people attending the clinic, I did have it in mind to contact Sporting Chance, as I knew they would probably have been understanding of my need for support, but reckoned that while the clinic was able to accommodate footballers with problems, some of whom were on contracts worth thousands of pounds a week, they would probably not be able to support someone associated with karate who also had a

spinal injury. Similarly, while spinal units now provided counselling as part of the rehabilitation process, I knew from past experience that the spinal unit at Salisbury would consider the needs of the newly injured more pressing, in addition to which, the problems I had were not really associated with my spinal injury. This, combined with the Spinal Injuries Association then not having a counselling service, and those 'Little Britain' sketches mocking counselling, rightly or wrongly had me avoiding it.

My symptoms thankfully subsided with time, though I would never be completely free of them, and I suppose, with the

At Regain's Sports Award lunch in 2007 with my sister.

combination of my injury and everything else I had been through in life, it was incredible that I not had such an episode earlier, especially as the psychological pain associated with my childhood problems would often be more acute than the physical pain associated with my spinal injury. I was therefore advised to take a new tack with the work I had started to do in the hospitality industry, and while this would be less beneficial financially, it would give me greater peace of mind. I also continued to gain various prizes for charities including Hospitality Action. This involvement proved helpful when my garage had to be extended to accommodate my new Motability vehicle and Hospitality Action were able to fund the extension.

I had not needed any assistance from the charity since its initial support over 20 years before, and it was gratifying that they were able to help out, especially as the industry was still close to my heart. Likewise, knowing many of the added complications and burdens of ageing while also being spinally injured, and how other things in life can bring different problems, it was also gratifying to know that support from the charity may also be available later in life or in other times of need. I also received wonderful support from Regain when I needed specialist equipment designed to help with ageing as a tetraplegic, and this, combined with an annual invitation to the Regain Sports Award luncheon, rekindled my desire to take on the book project I had considered some years earlier.

I had also recently lost two close friends in a short period of time due to heart attacks, one of them our 'Leader'. My tetraplegic friend from Newquay also died suddenly some months later. This made me realise how short life can be, and that I needed to make the most of it while I could.

I contacted the friend who had offered to support my book project earlier and we discussed things over a meal at Jamie Oliver's Fifteen restaurant in Cornwall, based at Watergate Bay. I had surfed many times at the beach as a youngster, the restaurant ironically having been built above the beach café originally owned by my first karate instructor. The food was superb, but my friend could see I was having difficulties eating it, the same problems as other disabled people eating out encountered. My friend thankfully agreed to support the idea I had in mind, which would result in the production of this book.

I began contacting various chefs, and while it may have seemed that this was just another of my wild schemes, I had some fantastic responses. Regardless of the fact that I would enter my 30th year as a tetraplegic during the compilation of this book, I feel extremely grateful for all the support I have received over the years. I have met some amazing people, some of whom have led incredible lives despite being tetraplegic and a few of

Party games and celebrations during the week of my 50th birthday with two former PA/carers, now friends, from Japan.

whom are featured in this book. I have also met many other disabled people who have achieved great things, and whilst my life, both as an able-bodied and disabled person, has been something of a roller-coaster ride, I feel privileged that my many dark moments have been offset by the superb support I have received.

I by no means feel that my accident was one of the best things that ever happened to me, as I'm sure I would have seen a lot more of the world as a chef or doing karate, and gone on to even greater things in either field. I also wish I was still able to do many of the things that I took for granted prior to my accident. However, I have achieved things I never imagined possible following my accident and am grateful that no one 'flipped the switch', so to speak, while I was in ICU in Bermuda.

I have been blessed to see two 'step-daughters' grow from teenagers to lovely women, and to see their children grow up, all of them lovingly calling me 'Pappy'. I have also been lucky enough to see a niece and a nephew grow up, the latter emulating my agility in karate by becoming a ballet dancer travelling the world in various shows for Matthew Bourne's *New Adventures Company*, as well as having seen other family members achieve good things.

I have also met some lovely PA/carers over the years, some of whom have become lifelong friends with me sort of becoming an 'Uncle David' to them, and though it would have been great to have been able to visit some of them in their own countries, two girls very kindly came all the way from Japan to celebrate my 50th birthday.

I also feel fortunate that while I may no longer live with my ex-partner she remains my principal carer and in many respects my best friend, which in turn gives quality and reliability even if things are not always rosy in the garden, so to speak! One reason for this is that ageing and caring do not go hand in hand, especially for someone whose appearance very much belies their years. She has also given great support to some of my PA/carers and has become lifelong friends with them. Support from various PA/carers and others over the years, while it may not always have run smoothly, as with life in general, has enabled me to do most of the things mentioned in

Taking my dog, Milly, for a walk around Charlestown Harbour.

this introduction, in conjunction with my Motability vehicles, especially the drive-from-wheelchair vehicles.

While our original dog sadly passed away, my ex-partner and I now share another Cavalier King Charles spaniel who gives a lot of love, and while it would be nice to meet another 'special lady', I sometimes feel that my life is too complicated and busy – but hey ho, who knows?

Over the last few years, with the support of friends, I have also been fortunate enough to see Truro City win the FA Vase at the new Wembley Stadium and to see Plymouth Argyle play Arsenal in the FA Cup at the superb

Emirates Stadium, although on both occasions we spent so much time in pubs and bars that I saw hardly anything of the surroundings! The game at the Emirates was really only made possible with the support of the police, who, with friends, helped lift me and my wheelchair up the stairs of the train station, which was not as wheelchair accessible as I had been led to believe! Similarly, I have been able to take short holidays in Yorkshire thanks to the support of my sister and her family, my sister having been most supportive of me over the last few years in many aspects of life.

In 2008 I took my first holiday abroad in 15 years, as a friend had built a wheelchair-accessible house in Cyprus. Other friends have also been supportive of late in different ways, and this, along with all the other support I have received in the past, has been very much appreciated. In conclusion, I hope this book will not only help chefs but also others in the hospitality industry understand some of the problems faced by disabled people eating

With friends at the 2009 Bouncers' Ball in Newquay.

At Hospitality Action's ball with Penny Moore, chief executive, HA.

that during the research and compilation of this book I was able to attend both Hospitality Action's ball at Grosvenor House and a fundraising dinner for HA cooked by the finalists of 'The Great British Menu', the latter again being made possible thanks to the Copthorne Tara (*Millennium & Copthorne Hotels*) kindly offering complimentary accommodation. Similarly, thanks to the Thistle Marble Arch (*Thistle Hotels*) in London and the Norfolk Royale *(Peel Hotels)* in Bournemouth kindly offering complimentary accommodation, I was able to attend Hotelympia 2010 and the Bournemouth Hotel & Catering Show and in turn meet some of the chefs who contributed recipes to this book. It was also great during the compilation of this book to attend the British Karate Federation's International Open in Glasgow, thanks in part to the support of Holiday Inn Hotels. While at the BKF's tournament it was great to be introduced to some faces from the past, like Billy Brennan and others from my own time doing karate, who I have great respect for. Similarly, thanks to the kindness of Mike Billman, BKF Board member, chairman of the European Technical Commission, member of the WKF World Technical Commission and member of the European Sports Commission, it was

out, and that it will also raise money for my two chosen charities. I also hope that it will be possible to produce a similar book in the future to help others, that the rest of my life will not be such a roller-coaster ride and that it will be possible for me to see some more of the world. In addition, I hope that I am able to stay in my own home with the same level of care and support that I have been used to for numerous years and, should I encounter unbearable problems and pain later in life, that my life will not be continued for ethical and moral reasons. Likewise, I hope it may be possible to rekindle my previous website project to enable others in a similar situation to myself to discover and enjoy more of the beautiful county of Cornwall. I feel privileged to live in such a lovely county, but it would be great if it could be made more accessible wherever possible.

The hospitality industry is a great one to be involved in and I feel fortunate

At the British Karate Federation's International Open with Billy Brennan, 8th Dan, and Mike Billman, 8th Dan

great to be introduced to latterday top class coaches and previous world champions such as Willie Thomas, Gerry Fleming and Craig Burke. Likewise, it was great to see other top class practitioners from around the world taking part in the Kumite and Kata sections, as it was the first time I had been to a major karate or martial arts tournament in over 25 years. In turn, it was superb to see so many youngsters now participating in a karate tournament and also showing great respect to their competitors, instructors and judges. When I started karate you were only allowed to train if you were in your teenage years, with many participants having to add a few years to their age in order to join a class! The most pleasing part of the tournament, though, was to watch the disability Kata event and see how people with disabilities also showed the same amount of respect, enthusiasm and etiquette as their able-bodied counterparts. Similarly, I was later

able to attend a fundraising dinner for Help for Heroes, and while the chefs who cooked the earlier meal at HA's fundraising dinner were most of the chefs that cooked the 'Great British Menu' banquet for troops coming home from Afghanistan and produced a similar menu, I still needed some assistance with my meal. No doubt very severely injured service personnel could possibly have encountered similar problems. Looking at the bigger picture and including diners who have arthritis, who are stroke victims, who are blind or visually impaired, and taking into account an increasingly aging population and all the other disabling illnesses, the number of people encountering similar problems to my own when eating out, I suspect, is extremely high. Also, as I and many others have had to fight to rebuild our lives after a disabling injury or illness, when life does get back on the straight and narrow, so to speak, the last thing we want is to have to struggle to gain access to a restaurant or a table when hoping for an enjoyable time out. Likewise, people do not always want to struggle with food that has been presented in a glamorous way but with no thought for those with limited dexterity. At Hotelympia it was pleasing to see that Le Salon Culinaire now included an Ability Award whereby disabled or disadvantaged people were able to showcase their cooking skills. With the 2012 Olympics and Paralympics set to be the greatest sporting events to happen in Great

Britain for many years, it would be great if Le Salon Culinaire and other cookery competitions nationally and at catering colleges, etc., could include an Accessibility Award. This could then showcase chefs' cooking skills in catering for diners with limited dexterity or other problems and so prepare chefs for the likes of the 2012 Paralympics and Regain's Sports Award luncheons. It was

With Albert Roux at the 2010 Restaurant Show.

also superb, nearing the completion of this introduction, thanks to the Holiday Inn London – Kensington Forum, to be able to attend the Restaurant Show and gain further sponsorship for Hospitality Action and Regain and again meet some of the chefs who have contributed recipes. Similarly, it was great to be able to attend the Craft Guild of Chefs awards night thanks to the Park Plaza Westminster Bridge hotel offering complimentary accommodation, and also to be invited to the Cornish Challenge event at Camborne College. At the Restaurant Show it was also great to meet Albert Roux, who, although he was probably unaware of who I was, still remained a true gent, as he had been in the past when he, along with many others in London, supported the Churchill's original fundraising campaign for me many years ago. The chefs' community, like the martial arts community, while they may have their different associations, person-

alities and rivalries, etc, have often left those to one side when supporting me with various things over the years, such as this book. As such I am extremely grateful to everyone who contributed to the book or who offered to contribute earlier. At the Restaurant Show it was also amazing to see the World Chocolate Masters competition, even though I only managed to take in a few snippets of the first day of the contest. The competition seemed light years away from the moulded chocolates, petit fours and pastries that we used to produce at the Churchill and elsewhere over 30 years before.

Although involvement in the hospitality industry can be rewarding, the combination of hard work and hard play can have life-changing consequences, as I know from my own experiences and from the experiences of others. As in many other walks of life, those working in hospitality are often involved in it their entire lives – in many instances working long hours for low pay – and this can cause problems later in life. In a strange way being tetraplegic has given me a bit of insight into such problems and the need for support. Similarly, there are many other disabling illnesses and life crises that may require someone to seek support. As mentioned earlier, while I was in some ways badly let down by the hospitality industry after my accident, with support from the Churchill Hotel and Hospitality Action, and from many others in the industry and elsewhere, I was able to rebuild my life. Since my accident 30 years ago, Hospitality Action has continued to support those in need from the industry in a multitude of ways. Demand for help grows year on year and with many people suffering from similar and other incapacitating conditions, it is hoped that those who already support Hospitality Action continue to do so, while those in the industry who may not have considered supporting Hospitality Action in the past seriously consider doing so in the future. It is the only benevolent association in the industry, so the more support it can offer its beneficiaries the better! Before my accident sport played an important part in my life, and though my spinal injury largely precludes my taking part in various sports, I and

others, able-bodied and disabled alike, get a great deal of enjoyment from watching it. While involvement in sport can also have devastating consequences, as you will see from the Dinner Party section of this book, with the right support and understanding, most things in life can still be accomplished and some amazing things achieved. Again, it is hoped that those who take part in sports consider supporting Regain, as anyone suffering a spinal injury in a sporting accident can require a great deal of support. I have always found humour to be one of the best ways of dealing with the consequences of my spinal injury and with life in general. If I, therefore, had to choose my own dinner party guests, apart from sporting stars or other icons, for diversity, culture and humour I would choose Billy Connolly, Robson Green and Dawn French, along with Paul Whitehouse in various guises to serve each course.

Finally, I hope this book makes for an interesting read whether or not you are involved in the hospitality industry or in sport, or just like watching it. In turn, I hope whether or not you are a disabled person or the loved one of a disabled person that you enjoy making or eating some of the dishes.

Bon appetit!

Index to the introduction

Action For Charity
New Court House, New Street, Lymington,
Hampshire, SO41 4BQ
Tel: 0845 408 2698
email: events@actionforcharity.co.uk
web: www.actionforcharity.co.uk

Apple Computers UK
Hollyhill Industrial Estate, Hollyhill, Cork,
Republic of Ireland
Tel: 0800 048 0408
web: www.apple.com/uk

Ark Foundation
62 Britton Street, London EC1M 5UY
Tel: 020 3004 5500   Fax: 020 7253 2094
email: info@hospitalityaction.org.uk
web: www.hospitalityaction.org.uk

Arsenal
Highbury House, 75 Drayton Park,
London, N5 1BU
Tel: 0844 931 2211
email: communications@arsenal.co.uk
web: www.arsenal.com

ASDA
ASDA House, Southbank, Great Wilson Street,
Leeds, LS11 5AD
Tel: 0844 481 5000
email: customer.services@asda.co.uk
web: www.asda.com

The Back Up Trust
Jessica House,
Red Lion Square,
191 Wandsworth High Street, SW18 4LS
Tel: 020 8875 1805   Fax: 020 8870 3619
web: www.backuptrust.org.uk

Bedruthan Steps Hotel
Mawgan Porth, Cornwall, TR8 4BU
Tel: 01637 860555
email: stay@bedruthan.com
web: www.bedruthan.com

Bournemouth Hotel & Catering Show
Optimus Events Ltd, CEM Group, Smugglers Way,
Hurn Lane, Ashley, Dorset, BH24 2AG
Tel: 01425 485040   Fax: 01425 483573
email: anna@hotel-expo.co.uk
web: www.hotel-expo.co.uk

British Airways
Tel: 0844 493 0 787
web: www.britishairways.com

British Karate Federation
email: info@britishkaratefederation.gb.com
web: www.britishkaratefederation.co.uk

Bujinkai Karate Association
Hazel Grove Civic Hall,
London Road, Hazel Grove,
Stockport, SK3 9RQ
Tel: 0161 480 9824
email: bujinkaikarate@yahoo.com
web: www.bujinkai.co.uk

Caterer & Hotelkeeper
web: www.caterersearch.com

Centre for Accessible Environments
70 South Lambeth Road, Vauxhall,
London SW8 1RL
Tel: 020 7840 0125   Fax: 020 7840 5811
email: info@cae.org.uk
web: www.cae.org.uk

Chelsea Football Club
Stamford Bridge, Fulham Road,
London SW6 1HS
Tel: 0871 984 1955
web: www.chelseafc.com

Chester Boyd
13 Devonshire Square,
London, EC2M 4TH
Tel: 020 7871 0577
email: enquire@chesterboyd.com
web: www.chesterboyd.com

City & Guilds
1 Giltspur Street, London EC1A 9DD
Tel: 0844 543 0000   Fax: 0207 294 2400
web: www.cityandguilds.com

Community Service Volunteers (CSV)
237 Pentonville Road, London N1 9NJ
Tel: 020 7278 6601
web: www.csv.org.uk

Compass Group UK & Ireland
Rivermead, Oxford Road, Denham,
Uxbridge UB9 4BF
Tel: 0189 5554 554
web: www.compass-group.co.uk

Copthorne Tara Hotel
Scarsdale Place, Kensington, London, W8 5SR
Tel: 020 7937 7211   Fax: 020 7937 7100
email: reservations.tara@millenniumhotels.co.uk
web: www.millenniumhotels.co.uk

Cornish Pirates
Westholme, Alexandra Road, Penzance,
Cornwall TR18 4LY
Tel: 01736 331961   Fax: 01736 335319
web: www.cornish-pirates.com

Cornwall Blind Association
Newham Road, Truro, Cornwall TR1 2DP
Tel: 01872 261110   Fax: 01872 222349
web: www.cornwallblind.org.uk

Cornwall College – St Austell
Tregonissey Road, St Austell, PL25 4DJ
Tel: 01726 226626
email: info@st-austell.ac.uk

Cornwall Mobility Centre
Tehidy House, Royal Cornwall Hospital, Truro,
Cornwall TR1 3LJ
Tel: 01872 254920   Fax: 01872 254921
email: mobility@rcht.cornwall.nhs.uk
web: www.cornwallmobilitycentre.co.uk

Craft Guild of Chefs
1 Victoria Parade, Sandycombe Road,
Richmond, Surrey TW9 3NB
web: www.craftguildofchefs.com

David Croft Trust Fund
c/o Chadwicks Accountants,
16A Menston Old Lane,
Burley in Wharfedale,
West Yorkshire, LS29 7QQ
Tel: 01943 862870   Fax: 01943 862872

Disability Cornwall
Units 1G & H Guildford Road Industrial Estate,
Guilford Road, Hayle
Cornwall, TR27 4QZ
Tel: 01736 759500
email: info@disabilitycornwall.org.uk
web: www.disabilitycornwall.org.uk

The Eden Project
Bodelva, Cornwall, PL24 2SG,
Tel: 01726 811 911
email: salesreferrals@edenproject.com
web: www.edenproject.com

England Karate Federation
EKF, PO Box 4372, Hornchurch,
Essex, RM12 9BN
Tel: 07590 632269
email: admin@englishkaratefederation.com
web: www.englishkaratefederation.com

Fifteen Cornwall
On The Beach, Watergate Bay,
Cornwall, TR8 4AA
Tel: 01637 861000
web: www.fifteencornwall.co.uk

Grosvenor House, A JW Marriott Hotel
Park Lane, London, W1K 7TN
Tel: 0207 499 6363   Fax: 44 207 6299337
web: www.marriott.co.uk

Headland Hotel
Fistral Beach, Newquay TR7 1EW
Tel: 01637 872211   Fax: 01637 872212
web: www.headlandhotel.co.uk

Help For Heroes
Unit 6, Aspire Business Centre, Ordnance Road,
Tidworth, Hants, SP9 7QD
Tel: 0845 673 1760
web: www.helpforheroes.org.uk

Hilton Hotels
Maple Court, Central Park, Reeds Crescent,
Watford WD24 4QQ
Tel: 0207 856 9471
email: press.office@hilton.com
web: www.hilton.co.uk

Holiday Inn Hotel & Resorts
Tel: 0871 423 4896
web: www.holidayinn.com

**Holiday Inn – London Kensington
Forum Hotel**
97 Cromwell Road, London, SW7 4DN
Tel: 0871 942 9100
web: www.hikensingtonforumhotel.co.uk

Holiday Property Bond (HPB)
HPB House, Newmarket, Suffolk CB8 8EH
Tel: 0800 230 0391
web: www.hpb.co.uk

Hotel Bristol
Narrowcliff, Newquay,
Cornwall, TR7 2PQ
Tel: 01637 875181   Fax: 01637 879347
email: info@hotelbristol.co.uk
web: www.bw-hotelbristol.co.uk

Hotelympia
Fresh RM, 9 Manchester Square,
London, W1U 3PL
Tel: 0207 886 3066
web: www.hotelympia.com

Hyatt Regency London – The Churchill
30 Portman Square, London, W1H 7BH
Tel: 0207 486 5800   Fax: 0207 486 1255
email: london.churchill@hyatt.com
web: www.hyatt.com

Huntleigh Healthcare
ArjoHuntleigh, 310-312 Dallow Road, Luton
Bedfordshire LU1 1TD
Tel: 01582 745700   Fax: 01582 745745
web: www.arjohuntleigh.co.uk

International Paralympic Committee (IPC)
Adenauerallee 212-214, 53113

Bonn, Germany
Tel: 49 228 2097 200
Fax: 49 228 2097 209
email: info@paralympic.org
web: www.paralympic.org

International World Games Association
Patsy Dew, Manager, 10 Lake Circle,
Colorado Springs, CO 80906, USA
Tel: 001 719 471 8096
Fax: 001 719 471 8105
email: info@worldgames-iwga.org
web: www.worldgames-iwga.org

Ishinryu Karate Association
email: information@ishinryu.org
web: www.ishinryu.org

Le Salon Culinaire
c/o 122 Starbold Crescent, Knowle, Solihull,
West Midlands B93 9LA
Tel:/Fax: 01564 776842
mob: 07778 311522
email: peter@salonculinaire.co.uk
web: www.hotelympia.com/salon
web: www.hospitalityshow.co.uk

Mawgan Porth Pools-Lake
Retorrick Mill, Newquay, Cornwall TR8 4BH
Tel:/Fax: 01637 860770
email: info@mawganporthpools-lake.co.uk
web: www.mawganporthpools-lake.co.uk

**Millennium and Copthorne Hotels
at Chelsea Football Club**
Stamford Bridge, Fulham Road,
London SW6 1HS
Tel: 020 7565 1400   Fax: 020 7565 1450
email: reservations.chelsea@millennium
hotels.co.uk

Millennium Hotels and Resorts
Tel: 0800 414741
web: www.millenniumhotels.com

Motability
Motability Operations, City Gate House, 22
Southwark Bridge Road,
London, SE1 9HB

Tel: 0845 456 4566
web: www.motability.co.uk

National Spinal Injuries Centre
Stoke Mandeville Hospital, Mandeville Road,
Aylesbury, Bucks, HP21 8AL
Tel: 01296 315000
web: www.buckinghamshirehospitals.nhs.uk

New Adventures (Dance Company)
c/o Sadler's Wells, Rosebery Avenue,
London, EC1R 4TN
Tel:/Fax: 020 7713 6766
email: info@new-adventures.net
web: www.new-adventures.net

The O2 (Arena)
The Studio, The O2,
London, SE10 0DX
Tel: 0208 463 2000
email: customerservices@theo2.co.uk
web: www.theo2.co.uk

Park Plaza Westminster Bridge
200 Westminster Bridge Road,
London SE1 7UT
Tel: 0844 415 6790
web: www.parkplaza.com

P&O Cruises
Carnival House, 100 Harbour Parade,
Southampton SO15 1ST
Tel: 0845 678 00 14   Fax: 023 8065 7030
web: www.pocruises.com

Plymouth Argyle Football Company Ltd
Home Park, Plymouth, Devon, PL2 3DQ
Tel: 01752 606167   Fax: 01752 606167
email: argyle@pafc.co.uk
web: www.pafc.co.uk

Queens Park Rangers Football Club
Loftus Road, South Africa Road, Shepherds Bush,
London W12 7PA
Tel: 0208 743 0262
web: www.qpr.co.uk

RAC
RAC Motoring Services, 8 Surrey Street, Norwich,

Norfolk NR1 3NG
Tel: 0844 891 3111
web: www.rac.co.uk

RADAR: The Disablility Network
12 City Forum, 250 City Road,
London, EC1V 8AF
Tel: 0207 250 3222   Fax: 0207 250 0212
email: radar@radar.org.uk
web: www.radar.org.uk

RAF Disabled Holiday Trust
Miss B Tomkins, 12 Park Crescent,
London, W1B 1PH
Tel: 0207 3073 303
email: admin@rafddht.org.uk
web: www.rafddht.org.uk

The Rocco Forte Collection
70 Jermyn Street, London SW1Y 6NY
Tel: 0207 321 2626   Fax: 0207 321 2424
email: enquiries@roccofortecollection.com
web: www.roccofortecollection.com

Salisbury District Hospital
Odstock Road, Salisbury, Wiltshire, SP2 8BJ
Tel: 01722 336262
email: customercare@salisbury.nhs.uk
web: www.salisbury.nhs.uk

Savoy Educational Trust
Queens House,
55-56 Lincoln's Inn Fields,
London, WC2A 3BH
Tel: 0207 269 9692   Fax: 0207 269 9694
email: info@savoyeducationaltrust.org.uk
web: www.savoyeducationaltrust.org.uk

Savoy – A Fairmont Managed Hotel
The Strand, London, WC2R 0EU
Tel: 0207 836 4343   Fax: 0207 420 2398
email: savoy@fairmont.com
web: www.fairmont.com/savoy

Savoy Grill
Strand, London, United Kingdom, WC2R 0EU
Tel: 0207 592 1600
email: savoy@gordonramsay.com
web: www.gordonramsay.com/thesavoygrill

Southern Spinal Injuries Trust
21 Chipper Lane, Sailsbury, Wiltshire, SP1 1BG
Tel: 07935 054 622
email: info@ssit.org.uk
web: www.ssit.org.uk

Spinal Injuries Association
SIA House, 2 Trueman Place, Oldbrook, Milton Keynes, MK6 2HH
Tel: 0845 678 6633   Fax: 0845 070 6911
email: sia@spinal.co.uk
web: www.spinal.co.uk

Sporting Chance Clinic
Crouch House, Champneys Forest Mere, Liphook, Hants, GU30 7QJ
Tel: 0870 2200714
email: info@sportingchanceclinic.com
web: www.sportingchanceclinic.com

Thistle Hotels
web: www.thistle.com

The Norfolk Royale Hotel
Richmond Hill, Bournemouth, Dorset, BH2 6EN
Tel: 01202 551 521
web: www.peelhotels.co.uk

Thistle Marble Arch
Bryanston Street, London, W1H 7EH
Tel: 0871 376 9027   Fax: 0871 376 9127
web: www.thistle.com

TJ International
Trecerus Industrial Estate, Padstow, Cornwall, UK, PL28 8RW
Tel: 01841 532691   Fax: 01841 532862
email: sales@tjinternational.ltd.uk
web: www.tjinternational.ltd.uk

Tourism For All
Shap Road Ind. Estate, Shap Road, Kendal, Cumbria, LA9 6NZ

Tel: 0845 124 9971   Fax: 01539 735567
email: info@tourismforall.org.uk
web: www.tourismforall.org.uk

Trusthouse Charitable Foundation
65 Leadenhall Street, London, EC3A 2AD
Tel: 020 7264 4990
www.trusthousecharitablefoundation.org.uk

Truro City Football Club
31 Lemon Street, Truro, Cornwall, TR1 2LS
Tel: 01872 278000   Fax: 01872 275458
email: enquiries@trurocityfc.co.uk
web: www.trurocityfc.co.uk

VIP International
VIP House, 17 Charing Cross Road, London, WC2H 0QW
email: vip@vipinternational.co.uk
web: www.vipinternational.co.uk

Wembley Stadium
Wembley National Stadium Ltd, Wembley, London, HA9 0WS
Tel: 0844 980 8001   Fax: 020 8795 5050
web: www.wembleystadium.com

Williams F1 Conference Centre
Station Road, Grove Oxfordshire OX12 0DQ
Tel: 01235 777900   Fax: 01235 777183
web: www.williamsf1conferences.com

World Karate Federation
email: secretariat@wkf.net
web: www.wkf.net

WUKO – World Union of Karate-do Organizations
Rua João Cachoeira no. 519, Itaim Bibi, São Paulo, Brazil, CEP. 04535-002
Tel: 55 11 3078.6014   Fax: 55 11 3168.7249
email: admin@WUKF-karate.org
web: www.wukokarate.org

Index of recipes

Starters

Main courses

Index of recipes

Beetroot salad with walnuts

Contributed by **Mark Hix**   Supported by

About Mark: A celebrated food writer and renowned restaurateur, Mark won *Tatler's* Restaurateur of the Year in 2009. In 2007, after 17 years at Caprice Holdings as Chef Director, he started his own venture, and in 2008 opened two new restaurants: Hix Oyster & Chop House in London and Hix Oyster & Fish House in Lyme Regis. His first West-End restaurant, HIX, opened to critical acclaim in 2009. His latest restaurant, HIX Restaurant and Champagne Bar, opened in Selfridges, London, in 2010. In addition to a weekly column in the *Independent* and a monthly column in *Country Life*, Mark has also written nine cookbooks, his latest being *Hix Oyster and Chop House*. His book *British Seasonal Food* won cookery book of the year at the Guild of Food Writers. Mark has also won *GQ's* Chef of the Year Award and the Academy Award for Outstanding Contribution to London Restaurants. Mark's sporting interests are fishing and golf.

Serves: 2   **Preparation time:** 5 mins   **Cooking time:** 10 mins + 1 hr for beets

'A simple beetroot salad makes a great light starter for a dinner party and will look stunning if you are able to source different coloured beetroot varieties from a farmers' market or good greengrocer. Cook the different beets separately, as their cooking times will vary slightly, and because the red beetroot is likely to stain the others.'

Ingredients:
500–600g mixed young beetroot (red, golden and white or candy-striped)
salt and freshly ground black pepper
30g good quality shelled walnuts
1 tsp good quality Cornish sea salt
$^1/_2$ tbsp rapeseed oil
a couple of handfuls of small salad and herb leaves (silver sorrel, red chard, orach, pea shoots, chives, etc.), washed

For the dressing:
1 tbsp cider vinegar
1 tbsp light Suffolk mustard (or similar)
4 tsp rapeseed oil

Method:
Cook the beetroots separately in salted water for about an hour, depending on the variety and size, until they feel tender when pierced with a sharp knife. Drain and leave until cool enough to handle, then peel away the skins with your fingers, wearing rubber gloves to stop the red beetroot staining your hands. Preheat the oven to 180°C/gas 4. Toss the walnuts with the sea salt and rapeseed oil and spread out on a baking tray. Toast in the oven for 4–6 minutes, turning them once or twice, until lightly coloured. To make the dressing, whisk the ingredients together in a small bowl and season with salt and pepper to taste. Cut the beetroot into even-sized wedges or halves if they are small. Cut the red ones last so you don't stain the lighter coloured ones. Arrange the beetroots and salad leaves on plates, season lightly and spoon over the dressing. Scatter over the walnuts and serve.

Photo by Jason Lowe, from British Seasonal Food (Quadrille, rrp £25).

Roasted pepper tart (savoury tarte tatin)

Contributed by **Galton Blackiston**   Supported by

About Galton: Galton, along with his wife Tracy, owns Morston Hall Hotel on the North Norfolk coast, and has done so for over 17 years. Morston Hall has, for the last 10 years, held a Michelin star, and Galton has appeared on numerous TV programmes such as 'Great British Menu', 'Saturday Kitchen' and 'Market Kitchen', and is currently working on a new series – 'Put your menu where your mouth is'. Galton has produced three bestselling books, the latest of which, *Summertime*, was published in 2009. He is still playing competitive cricket, is an ambassador at Norwich City Football Club and occasionally hacks around a golf course (with a handicap of 18!!!). He also enjoys shooting in the company of friends and his dog Daisy, and is a very keen shot. He also gets immense pleasure watching the sporting achievements of his sons, Harry and Sam.

Serves: 6   **Preparation time:** 30 mins approx.   **Cooking time:** 25 mins

Ingredients:
4 each of red, yellow and orange peppers
olive oil and butter for frying the onions
3 red onions, peeled and sliced
25g (1 oz) basil leaves
6 tomatoes, skinned, deseeded and halved

homemade or good quality bought puff pastry
salt and pepper

You will also need a 20 cm (8 in) tarte tatin tin, sides buttered, with a circle of good quality greaseproof paper lining the base.

How to roast peppers
Everyone has their own way of removing skins from peppers. The method used here ensures the skins are wrinkled enough to remove, although some people prefer to place them under a grill or even use a blow torch.

Method:

To roast the peppers, pre-heat the oven to 220°C/425°F/gas 7 and lightly oil a baking tray. Halve the peppers and remove the seeds. Place the peppers cut side down on the baking tray, drizzle with oil and grate over some garlic (optional). Season with salt and pepper.

Cook on a low shelf for 10 minutes, turn the tray round and cook for a further 10 minutes. The skins of the peppers may be sufficiently wrinkled but should not be charred or shrunken.

Remove the peppers from the oven, place in a bowl and cover with clingfilm. After a few minutes, the steaming effect will allow you to slip the skins off easily. While they are roasting, add a little olive oil and butter to a hot frying pan. Turn the heat down and sauté the red onions, stirring occasionally, until softened and beginning to caramelise. Remove from the heat.

Pre-heat oven to 200°C/400°F/gas 6.

When the peppers are cool enough to handle, skin and halve. Arrange half the peppers in the base of the tarte tatin dish, skinned side down, pointing towards the centre and alternating red, yellow and orange slices. Sprinkle a third of

the basil leaves over the peppers. Repeat with the remaining peppers and more basil leaves, then season.

Place the tomato halves on top of the peppers, season well with salt and pepper and sprinkle with the remaining basil leaves. Finally, spread the cooked onions over the top.

Roll out the pastry. Cut out a circle just a little larger than the tarte tatin tin. Place this on top of the onions, tucking in the edges. Cut little holes in the pastry, then cook in the oven for about 25 minutes, or until the pastry is golden-brown.

Remove from the oven and allow to stand for 5 minutes before turning the tart out on to a large serving plate. Serve warm or cold.

Roast scallops with 'beans on toast', celeriac purée, white asparagus and vinaigrette with Jabugo ham

Contributed by **John Williams**   Supported by

About John: Having developed a passion for cookery at an early age, John's skills were honed at school and college. After gaining his City & Guilds he started at the Royal Garden, working his way up to Chef de Cuisine. There followed an impressive 18-year tenure with the Savoy Group. John, who works tirelessly to promote the education and training of chefs, is Executive Chairman of the Academy of Culinary Arts and a member of the Adopt a School Committee. This work resulted in John becoming Executive Chef of The Ritz in 2004 – the ultimate accolade for any British chef, The Ritz being the only hotel to hold the Royal Warrant from His Royal Highness The Prince of Wales. John's other accolades include an MBE for services to hospitality and a Catey Award. John's main sporting interest is golf, which he plays every week.

Serves: 2 **Preparation time:** 5 mins **Cooking time:** 10 mins

Ingredients:

10 large scallops
200g fresh broad beans
mint
olive oil
salt & sugar for seasoning
juice of 1 lemon
5 slices Poilaine bread
1 clove garlic
1 head celeriac
500 ml milk

500 ml cream
butter
10 spears white asparagus, blanched.
200g diced Jabugo ham
4 large carrots, finely diced
100g chopped parsley
4 shallots, finely diced
Cabernet Sauvignon vinegar
olive oil
chervil to garnish

Method, celeriac purée:

Top, tail and skin the celeriac and cut into large dice. Place into the pan with the milk and cream and season with salt. Bring to the boil and simmer until tender. Drain and place the celeriac into a blender with a little of the cooking liquor and some diced butter. Whizz until perfectly smooth (correct as you go with the cooking liquor). Season, pass and chill.

Jabugo vinaigrette:

Dice the Jabugo ham into small cubes. In a high-sided pan, render and soften it gently with olive oil. Mix in the diced shallot and carrot. Remove from the heat and allow to cool. Mix in, to taste, the Cabernet Sauvignon vinegar. Add the parsley. If too thick, thin with more olive oil and re-season with vinegar.

Broad bean mix

Blanch the beans in boiling seasoned water, refresh and de-shell. Place into a bowl with a touch of olive oil, salt and sugar. Crush with a fork and add lemon juice drop by drop. Add matchstick size strips of mint and check seasoning.

To finish the dish, toast the Poilaine under the grill and rub it once lightly with the peeled garlic clove. Cut into a neat, elegant rectangle. Cut the asparagus tip to the same length as the toast and slice the rest of the stem on the angle. Cook the scallops. Place a swipe of celeriac purée on the plate. Add a layer of crushed broad beans to the toast and top with the asparagus tip and a chervil sprig. Place the scallops onto the plate. Place the sliced asparagus around the plate along with the vinaigrette and garnish with more chervil, all similar to the plated dish in the photo.

Soy-glazed mackerel resting on an oriental salad

Contributed by **Martin Burge**

Supported by  **active hands**

About Martin: Born in Bristol, Martin trained at Brunel Technology College. His first job was at the Royal Crescent in Bath. Following a move to London he worked at the Mirabelle restaurant, Pied à Terre, and later with Raymond Blanc at Le Manoir aux Quat' Saisons, Oxford. Martin then went to work at L'Ortolan with John Burton-Race and later at the Landmark Hotel, Marylebone, London, achieving two Michelin stars in just a year. In 2003 Martin returned to the West Country as Head Chef at Whatley Manor, Wiltshire. Here he oversees both the fine dining restaurant – The Dining Room – and the brasserie-style Le Mazot. In the last eight years, among numerous accolades, he attained his first Michelin star in 2005 and a second in 2009. Martin participated in the semi-finals of 'MasterChef: The Professionals' 2010 and has been a judge in the finals since 2008. Relais & Châteaux awarded Martin the 'Grands Chefs Trophy' 2011. Martin's sporting interests include cycling, cardio and weight training. His sporting motto, 'you are only as good as your team', also resounds in his kitchen.

Serves: 4 **Preparation time:** 30 mins **Cooking time:** 4 mins

Ingredients for the pickled ginger:
75g peeled sliced ginger
1 lemon
700 ml cold water
12.5g + 60g caster sugar
200 ml rice wine vinegar
60g caster sugar

For the mackerel:
2 whole filleted, pin boned and skinned mackerel (your fishmonger will do this)
5g toasted sesame seeds

For the oriental salad:
¹/₂ cucumber

150g frozen edamame or broad beans
4 red radishes
50g mixed baby leaf lettuce
20g pickled ginger
prepared oriental dressing

For the oriental dressing:
75 ml rice wine vinegar
75 ml honey
100 ml peanut oil

For the soy glaze:
100 ml ketjap manis
10 ml light soy sauce

Method:

For the pickled ginger, cut the lemon into quarters, peel and slice ginger thinly. Squeeze the juice from $1/4$ lemon onto the ginger to stop it oxidising. In a saucepan, place the ginger, 350 ml cold water, 12.5g sugar and the juice from $1/4$ lemon. Bring to the boil then strain. Repeat the process. In a separate pan mix the vinegar and 60g sugar, add the strained ginger and bring to the boil. Allow to cool and refrigerate until ready to use.

For the dressing, whisk together the honey and vinegar, slowly add the peanut oil until incorporated and set aside until ready to use.

For the soy glaze, mix the two ingredients.

Wash the salad in cold water and drain until ready to use. Peel and halve the cucumber. Scrape out the cucumber seeds and discard. Cut the cucumber into two inch batons about as thick as a pencil. Meanwhile, defrost the beans in cold water. Remove beans from the pods and skin from the beans. Cut the bottom off the radishes, discard the sprout. Slice radishes thinly.

Lightly toast the sesame seeds and set aside.

Place mackerel on a non-stick tray flat side up. Heavily brush the soy glaze over the fish and grill for 4 minutes, brushing with more glaze every 20-30 seconds so that it starts to thicken.

Mix the salad leaves, radish, drained ginger, beans and cucumber batons, lightly coat with the dressing and split evenly among four pasta bowls. Place the cooked mackerel on top and sprinkle with toasted sesame seeds.

Myburgh du Plessis, Network Book Publishing Ltd.

Marinated warm chicken liver pudding with wild mushrooms

Contributed by **Michael Kitts**

Supported by  collinsking & associates

About Michael: Michael began his career at Claridge's before moving to the Garrick Club. He then worked at London's Ritz Casino and InterContinental Hotel before moving to Bristol as Executive Chef for the Swallow Royal Hotel. Returning to London as Executive Chef for the Les Ambassadeurs Club, he then joined the Butler's Wharf Chef School as Culinary Director. Michael has had great success in international competitions, winning over 50 gold medals. He was a member of the gold-medal-winning Great Britain Culinary Olympics team in 1987, and the first recipient of the UK Craft Guild of Chefs competition Chef Award. He puts his competition experience to good use training others, and in 1994 teams he had trained won both junior and senior 'Grand Prix' at Hotelympia. In 1996 Michael was awarded the Prince Philip Special Award for services to the industry and his current role is Director of Culinary Arts at the Emirates Academy of Hospitality Management in Dubai. He is a moderate Spurs fan and enjoys golf and skiing.

Serves: 6 **Preparation time:** 2 hrs **Cooking time:** 25 mins

Ingredients:
200g chicken livers, sinew and any discoloured parts removed
200 ml milk

For the marinade:
1 medium garlic clove, sliced thinly
1 sprig thyme, leaves only
6 white peppercorns, crushed
50 ml extra virgin olive oil

For the pudding:
30g butter, melted
2 eggs
100 ml double cream
pinch freshly grated nutmeg,
salt and pepper

For the garnish:
20 Thai or baby asparagus tips, 5 cm long, blanched in boiling water for

1 min, then plunged in ice-cold water
100g mixed wild mushrooms prepared,
washed and dried (use trimmings for
sauce)
40g butter
10g shallots, finely chopped
small sprig rosemary, finely chopped
20 redcurrants, washed and dried on
kitchen paper
4 chervil sprigs

For the sauce:
20g butter
10g shallots, finely chopped
mushroom trimmings
100 ml double cream
75 ml chicken stock
salt and pepper

You will need:
4 timbale moulds, about 6 cm dia, 5 cm
deep, lightly buttered
4 bowl plates

Prior preparation of chicken livers:
Place the chicken livers into a bowl and
cover with the milk. Cover with plastic
wrap and leave in the refrigerator
overnight.

Discard the milk and pat dry the livers
with absorbent kitchen paper. They are
then ready for use.

To make the marinade:
Mix the marinade ingredients together
in a bowl, then coat the chicken livers in
the marinade, cover the bowl and place
in the fridge for 1 hour.

To make the pudding:
Remove the livers from the marinade,
discard the marinade.

Place the livers into a food processor/
liquidiser, add the remaining pudding
ingredients and blend for 3–4 minutes
until very smooth.

Pass the mixture through a fine sieve
into a clean bowl.

Pour the mixture into the buttered
timbale moulds.

Place the moulds into a shallow pan
(bain-marie) and carefully fill with hot
water to no more than halfway up the
moulds.

Cover with a lid or tin foil, place into
the oven gas 2/150°C for 25 minutes
or until firm to the touch, remove from
the oven and allow to stand for 1
minute.

To make the garnish:
Heat a non-stick pan, add the butter
and finely chopped shallots and cook
over a gentle heat for 2–3 minutes.

Add the rosemary and mushrooms,
increase the heat and cook for a further
minute. Season with salt and pepper.

Add the blanched asparagus and cook
for 1 minute.

To make the sauce:
Heat a non-stick pan, add half the
butter and finely chopped shallots and
cook for 2–3 minutes.

Add the mushroom trimmings, cook
for 2–3 minutes and add the chicken
stock.

Bring to the boil, then simmer until the stock has reduced by half.

Add the cream and again bring to the boil, reduce the heat and simmer for 2–3 minutes.

Season with salt and pepper.

Pour the mixture into a food processor/liquidiser and blend until smooth.

Add the remaining butter and blend for a further 10 seconds.

Season to taste.

To finish:
Carefully turn out the pudding onto the centre of the plate.

Arrange the mushrooms around the outside of the pudding, 5 pieces of asparagus and 5 pieces of redcurrant on each plate.

Drizzle the sauce over the mushrooms.

Garnish the pudding with the picked chervil and serve.

Chef's tip:
Place three sheets of kitchen paper under the timbale moulds in the bain-marie before filling with the hot water. This will ensure that they don't move around.

Cornish lamb with thyme and red wine gravy

Contributed by **Kevin Viner**   Supported by

About Kevin: Kevin has won some of Britain's most renowned professional cooking competitions, and was UK National Chef of the Year in 1998 and the AA's Chef of the Year in 1999. Also nominated as one of the 'Top ten chefs of the last decade' by the AA, Kevin was chef/proprietor of Pennypots Restaurant, the first Michelin starred restaurant in Cornwall and is now Executive Chef of Viners Bar & Restaurant at Summercourt in central Cornwall. The Michelin Guide awarded a 'Bib Gourmand' to Viners in 2010. Kevin was also a member of the British team of chefs that won gold medals in the World Culinary Olympics. He now judges competitions and in 2009 and 2010 was invited to act as Chairman of Judges at Hotelympia. He is passionate about coaching other chefs. Kevin's leisure interests include coastal walks in Cornwall with his wife and their three dogs, and scuba diving in tropical waters.

Serves: 6   **Preparation time:** 1 hour   **Cooking time:** 4 hours

Ingredients:
shoulder of new season Cornish lamb, boned, rolled and tied
loin of lamb, boned and trimmed
1 bottle red wine
3 cloves garlic
30g fresh thyme
4 bay leaves
100g chopped parsley
50 ml port
1 beef stock cube
salt and pepper
vegetables for pot roasting (all roughly chopped): 1 carrot, 1 celery stick,

1 small onion, $^1/_2$ leek
100g butter

Garnish vegetables:
Red pepper, deseeded and finely sliced, fried in olive oil; courgette, sliced, fried in olive oil; aubergine, sliced and cut into batons, fried in olive oil; 500g cherry tomatoes on the vine, roasted in the oven with garlic and fresh thyme; 500g new potatoes, boiled; baby leek, cut into batons, boiled

Method:

In a large casserole dish heat some olive oil. Brown the lamb on all sides and then remove.

Fry the vegetables until coloured and put the lamb back in.

Add half a bottle of red wine, the port, half the butter, a third of the thyme, parsley stalks, bay leaves, garlic cloves and seasoning. Cover and put in the oven for 4 hours at 120°C. Check and baste every 30 minutes.

When cooked, remove the dish from the oven and allow to cool slightly.

Butter the inside of a metal ring and sprinkle with chopped parsley. Then cut the shoulder and loin into bite-sized pieces. Place the cut shoulder on the plate, place the metal ring on top and insert the chopped loin, pressing down slightly before removing the ring.

Present in a way similar to that pictured below.

Turbot with ginger and thyme

Contributed by **James Tanner**   Supported by

About James: From a pocket money job preparing vegetables and washing up at the tender age of 12, James has never looked back, climbing the culinary ladder to the top! After completing a diploma course in hospitality, James's path has taken him through top kitchens in London, New York and throughout England. In 1999 he opened Tanners Restaurant, which has won Restaurant of the Year for England. This was followed by the Barbican Kitchen brasserie in 2006. For the last eight years James has graced our TV screens on national and international mainstream programmes promoting food and British produce. James's third book was published in 2010, and when not in the kitchen, his interests include snowboarding, art and motor sports.

Serves: 2 **Preparation time:** 5 mins **Cooking time:** 10 mins

Ingredients:
400 ml fresh fish stock
2 tsp chopped thyme
salt and freshly ground pepper
juice of ½ lemon

200g fresh egg tagliatelle
1 tsp chopped stem ginger in syrup
330g skinned turbot fillet
25g butter
2 large handfuls of fresh spinach

Method:
Pour the fish stock into a non-stick pan. Add the ginger and thyme. Cut the turbot into 2 inch pieces (mouth size pieces). Season the turbot with salt and freshly ground pepper and place the turbot in the fish stock. Cover the turbot with greaseproof paper, bring to a simmer and poach for 2 minutes. Remove the paper and simmer for a further 2 minutes.

Carefully remove the turbot from the poaching liquor and set aside, keeping it warm.

Over a low heat, mix the butter into the poaching liquor and add the lemon juice.

Meanwhile, heat the olive oil in a heavy-based saucepan. Put in the spinach, season with salt and freshly ground pepper and fry, stirring now and then, until the spinach is just wilted.

Bring a large saucepan of salted water to the boil. Put in the tagliatelle and cook until 'al dente' – a matter of minutes. Drain.

Serve the poached turbot on top of the sautéed spinach and tagliatelle and spoon over a little ginger and thyme sauce.

Recipe cooked, plated and photographed by Cornwall College – St Austell.

Seared red mullet with piperade

Contributed by **Chris Galvin**   Supported by

About Chris: Chris's career has spanned 30 years. Originally inspired by his grandmother's cooking, he began under Anthony Worrall-Thompson and then at The Ritz hotel in London under Michael Quinn. He teamed up again with Worrall-Thompson in New York as head chef at Menage à Trois, before returning to London. Later he joined Conran Restaurants, where he worked with Sir Terence Conran for ten years, one of the highlights being the launch of Orrery in 1997, which gained a Michelin star in 2000. He was later promoted to Chef Director of the group. In 2003 Chris became Executive Chef at The Wolseley. In September 2005 Chris and his brother Jeff opened their first solo venture, Galvin Bistrot de Luxe, and in May 2006 they launched Galvin at Windows, on the 28th Floor of the London Hilton on Park Lane. In November 2009 they moved into the City, opening La Chapelle and Café a Vin. Both La Chapelle and Galvin at Windows have been awarded Michelin stars. Chris's sporting interests are regular gym sessions and running, and he is involved in the annual Mayfair Park and Tower Race, raising money for his charity, The Galvin Chance, which helps disadvantaged youngsters obtain experience – and hopefully work – within the hospitality industry.

Serves: 4   **Preparation time:** 1 hr   **Cooking time:** 45 mins

Ingredients:
8 x 75–80g red mullets fillets, scaled and pin boned
2 tbsp olive oil
salt and pepper

Piperade:
50 ml olive oil
2 garlic cloves, peeled and crushed
2 peeled and thinly sliced onions
2 green peppers, seeded and cut into

fine strips
3 red peppers, seeded and cut into fine strips
salt and piment désplat (a type of paprika from the south west of France)
4 sprigs flat parsley, very roughly chopped
4 slices Bayonne ham cut in strips
20 Provençal black olives
2 tbsp extra virgin olive oil

Method:

First prepare the piperade by heating the olive oil and adding the garlic and onions, cooking slowly until soft and golden, then add the green peppers for 3–4 minutes, followed by the red peppers. Cook until soft and any resulting juices are reduced and incorporated back into the mix. Add the seasoning at this point.

Brush the red mullet with the olive oil and grill for 1–2 minutes until just cooked. Sprinkle with a few drops of lemon juice and a little salt.

Whilst the fish is grilling, place the Bayonne ham alongside under the grill until it starts just to curl; take care not to overcook and dry out.

Spoon the piperade into the centre of the plate, place the mullet on top then sprinkle with the ham, parsley and olives and a splash of olive oil.

Split lentil and spicy sausage stew

Contributed by **Gordon Ramsay**   Supported by

About Gordon: Scottish by birth, Gordon was brought up in Stratford-upon-Avon from the age of five. With an injury prematurely putting an end to any hopes of a promising career in football, he went back to college to complete a course in hotel management. Gordon's first years in the kitchen were spent training under culinary luminaries such as Marco Pierre White and Albert Roux, after which he moved to France. In 1993, he became chef of the newly opened Aubergine, which was later awarded two Michelin stars. In 1998 he set up his own restaurant, Gordon Ramsay, which was awarded three Michelin stars. Since then Gordon and his team have launched some of the world's most high profile restaurants, including the iconic Savoy Grill in London. He has also become a TV star in the UK and internationally and has published numerous books. He has run the London marathon on many occasions.

Serves: 4   **Preparation time:** 20 mins   **Cooking time:** 1 hr

Ingredients:
8 good quality pork or beef sausages
2–3 tbsp olive oil
2 medium onions, peeled and chopped
2–3 cloves garlic, peeled and chopped
2 tbsp sweet paprika
4 sticks celery, trimmed and finely chopped

2 red or yellow peppers, deseeded and finely chopped
500g lentils
1x 400g tin chopped tomatoes
1 tbsp Worcestershire sauce
2 litres chicken stock
small bunch of coriander and flat leaf parsley, chopped

Method:
Cut the sausages into fairly thick chunks about 2.5 cm long. Heat the oil in a large sauté pan or casserole and add the onions, garlic and paprika. Stir over medium heat for 3–4 minutes then add the sausages. Cook for a few minutes until the sausages are golden, and then add the celery, peppers and some seasoning. Sauté for 4–5 minutes until the peppers begin to soften.

Add the lentils, tomatoes and Worcestershire sauce and then pour in the stock. Reduce the heat and simmer for about 1–1$^{1}/_{2}$ hours until the lentils are soft and have absorbed most of the liquid. Scatter over the fresh herbs and serve immediately.

Posh scouse

Contributed by **Gareth Billington**   Supported by

About Gareth: Gareth started at South Cheshire College on a chefs' course. He served his apprenticeship at The Garrick Club, London, before moving on to the QE2 luxury cruise liner, then to the Mermaid Beach Club, Bermuda, and afterwards to the A Galeria Restaurant, Portugal. Since 2004 Gareth has been at Everton Football Club as Executive Head Chef, where he has won numerous awards for hospitality. Gareth is an ambassador for Springboard, a charitable organisation which spreads the word about careers in hospitality to the young, unemployed and disadvantaged. Gareth has trained many aspiring young chefs, many of whom have gone on to win national culinary competitions. Gareth loves red wine, football, travelling, golf and sitting on Caribbean beaches drinking mojitos and watching the ladies go by.

Serves: 4   **Preparation time:** 45 mins   **Cooking time:** 30 mins

Ingredients:
4x150g cannon of lamb
2 carrots
1 swede
2 potatoes
4 baby beetroots
4 shallots
1 savoy cabbage, shredded
approximately into 60 mm lengths and
5 mm widths.

For the sauce:
450 ml veal stock
1 shallot, roughly chopped
few sprigs of fresh thyme
few sprigs of fresh rosemary
150g redcurrant jelly
250 ml port

Method:
1. Peel and cut the carrots, swede and potatoes into 15 mm cubes, 8 cubes of each.
2. Lightly poach in veal stock. Drain, reserving the poaching liquor.
3. Peel and halve the shallots, lightly sauté in a little oil, drain and set aside.
4. Peel the baby beetroots, poach in salted water until tender, drain and set aside.
5. Season the lamb with salt and pepper.
6. To a hot pan add a dessert spoon of vegetable oil.
7. Carefully place the lamb in the pan.

Seal until slightly brown on all sides.

8. Drain the oil from the pan, place the lamb on an oven tray and place in the oven, preheated to 200°C, for 7 minutes.

9. To the pan in which the lamb was sealed add the port, rosemary, thyme and shallots. Reduce by three-quarters. Add the veal stock (used for poaching the vegetables) and redcurrant jelly. Reduce to a sauce consistency, then pass through a sieve, discarding the solids.

10. Add the carrot, swede, beetroots, shallots and potato to the hot sauce.

Gently simmer for 3 minutes.

11. Remove the lamb from the oven and allow to rest.

12. To salted simmering water add the savoy cabbage. When cooked, drain the cabbage and place it in the middle of the serving plate.

13. Place the sliced lamb on top of the cabbage.

14. Divide the vegetables equally and place around the cabbage.

15. Spoon the sauce over and around the vegetables.

16. Serve.

Hearty vegetarian bean stew

Contributed by **Mark Askew**   Supported by

T I B A R D
Wear *for*
Work

About Mark: Mark started his career in the North of England. A move to London in 1989 brought his first encounter with Gordon Ramsay when he took on a role as a Commis Chef at the Savoy Grill. He then worked alongside Pierre Koffmann, Michel Bourdin and Nico Ladenis. In 1992, Mark once again worked with Gordon at Aubergine and to further his skills he made the decision to move to France. He then returned to Aubergine as Head Chef and went on to work alongside Gordon at Restaurant Gordon Ramsay on Royal Hospital Road. Their hard work and determination was rewarded with a third Michelin Star in 2001, and these have been retained every year to date. Since 2001 Mark has acted as Executive Head Chef of Gordon Ramsay Holdings. Mark's sporting interests include cycling, and he does London to Brighton each year in support of the British Heart Foundation.

'I keep a large selection of both dried and canned beans in my cupboard. Canned beans need little pre-planning and make amazing nutritious and hearty stews. I've used a combination of chickpeas and cannellini, black eyed and haricot beans here, but almost any combination will work. I have kept this recipe vegetarian, but adding some spicy sausage or bacon would also be delicious. Top with a spoonful of sour cream or Greek yoghurt and a sprinkling of paprika.'

Serves: 4–6 **Preparation time:** 30 mins **Cooking time:** 30 mins

Ingredients:

500 ml vegetable stock
1 onion, finely chopped
1 leek, white part only, finely sliced
3 sticks celery, tough parts discarded, finely sliced
1 clove garlic, finely chopped
2 tbsp olive oil
1 large beef tomato, skinned, deseeded and roughly chopped
freshly ground pepper

1 tsp ground cumin
1 tsp paprika
freshly ground coriander seeds
3 sprigs thyme
2 bay leaves
300g each of cooked haricot beans, black-eyed beans, cannellini beans and chickpeas
handful fresh herbs, roughly chopped
125 ml sour cream or yoghurt
paprika, to dust

Method:

Bring the stock to the boil. Meanwhile, fry the onion, leek, celery and garlic in the oil for a few minutes until translucent but not coloured. Add the tomato and seasonings, cook for a further 2–3 minutes, then add the stock. Add the thyme and bay, adjust the seasoning, then simmer for 20 minutes. Add the beans, simmer for 3–4 minutes, then add herbs. Divide between 4 warmed serving bowls, top with sour cream, sprinkle with paprika and serve with plenty of crusty bread.

Recipe cooked, plated and photographed by Cornwall College – St Austell.

A simple fish stew

Contributed by **Mitch Tonks**   Supported by

About Mitch: When Mitch was young his sport was water-skiing, which was taught to him by his dad. By the time he was 12 he was into offshore ski racing, which in those days consisted of hanging on behind a boat for 50 miles, and he remembers some awful conditions. As the sport progressed boats got faster and he moved up the formulas and got to ski behind a 19' phantom with a 150hp engine – and boy did it go! The following year he moved up to formula 2 and an even bigger engine, and found that amazing, although at times scary. Mitch won a few races but didn't really have the bottle to reach the speeds of up to 90 miles an hour his competitors were getting to! It was time for him to retire and become a cook, but not before winning the junior British championship.

Serves: 4   **Preparation time:** 10 mins   **Cooking time:** 25 mins

For the aïoli:
2 egg yolks
1 tsp Dijon mustard
4 cloves of garlic, pasted
150 ml/5 fl oz good olive oil
juice of ¹/₂ lemon
sea salt

For the stew:
1 shallot, finely chopped
2 cloves garlic, chopped
olive oil
2 tomatoes, roughly chopped

pinch of saffron
3–4 sprigs of thyme
splash of Pernod or anise
splash of white wine
selection of fish – you can use anything, really, mussels, clams, gurnard, monkfish, wrasse, mullet (ask a fishmonger for some fish with all the shells or bones removed and cut into mouth sized pieces, if this helps)
sea salt
parsley or basil, chopped, for sprinkling on top

'After a day on the water a nice bowl of fish stew is just what you need, and this is a very easy recipe with spectacular results.'

To make the aïoli:

Put the egg yolks in a bowl with the mustard and garlic. Whilst whisking add the olive oil in a steady stream until a thick emulsion is formed. Add the lemon juice, season to taste.

To make the stew:

In a large pan, sweat the shallots and garlic in olive oil. Add the tomatoes, saffron and thyme and stir together.

Add the Pernod and tip the pan away from you, allowing it to burn off the alcohol. Add the wine and simmer gently for 2 minutes. Add the fish and add enough water just to cover it. Simmer for 8–10 minutes.
Remove the thyme and season.

Finally, sprinkle with fresh chopped herbs and accompany with bread and the rich, garlicky aïoli.

Photograph: Carlo Chinca.

Steamed hake supreme with a mussel broth and saffron aïoli

Contributed by **Grant Mather**   Supported by

About Grant: After initially training in Cornwall, Grant travelled to London, where he worked for several years in the West End. This included a good spell at the Dorchester under head chef Anton Mosimann. After that he moved north of the border, where he worked at one of Glasgow's leading restaurants. Grant finally returned to Cornwall, where he continued to work in good quality establishments and found time to marry and raise a family. In 2000 he entered further education and has now been teaching full time for eight years. He continues to work in education and hopes the new qualifications will give young chefs a far better grounding in their vocational development. Grant spent many years involved in the running of youth football in Cornwall, but his main sporting interest is now rugby.

Serves: 4   **Preparation time:** 45 mins   **Cooking time:** 10 mins

Ingredients:
4 x 3 oz hake supremes, scaled and pin-boned
1 pt shellfish stock
$^1/_2$ pt white wine or Noilly Prat
4 oz chilled butter
1 pt mussels
1 onion, finely diced
1 clove garlic, crushed
1 tbsp snipped chives

For the saffron aïoli:
30g chopped fresh garlic
2 anchovy fillets
2g saffron
3 egg yolks
450 ml olive oil
2 tbsp lemon juice
$^1/_2$ tbsp boiled water

Method:

Prepare fish and season lightly. Check and clean the mussels. Sweat the onion and garlic in the butter, add the mussels and cover for 1 minute. Add the wine and cook until the mussels have opened. Steam the hake. Remove the mussels from the pan, pull the meat from the shells and return the meat to the broth. Add the butter and chives.

Place a spoonful of broth in a bowl and sit a supreme of hake on the top. Dress with a quenelle of aïoli and serve.

For the aïoli, infuse the saffron in the water and let stand. Blitz the anchovy and garlic to a paste, then mix the egg, anchovy, lemon and saffron water in a bowl. Slowly drizzle in the oil, whisking all the time. Check the seasoning and consistency. Refrigerate until required.

Recipe cooked, plated and photographed by Cornwall College – St Austell.

Slow-cooked belly of pork casserole

Contributed by **Paul Ainsworth**   Supported by

About Paul: Paul was born in Southampton and grew up in his family-run guesthouse. He studied catering at Southampton College. At the age 18 he made his way to London and spent two years with Gary Rhodes at Rhodes in the Square, three years at Royal Hospital Road with Gordon Ramsay and three years with Marcus Wareing at Petrus. In 2005 Paul's career changed dramatically when he moved to Padstow, Cornwall. He set up a restaurant with some friends and in 2008 took sole occupancy, creating a dining experience that won over the locals with his hearty value-for-money menu. Paul raises money for the Padstow lifeboat every year with his special RNLI lunch menus. In May 2010 he began to focus his interest on rustic Italian style food with his second restaurant, Rojano's. He always had a desire to have this type of restaurant to allow him to create dishes to be shared. He loves living in Padstow with his wife; they have a very big family in Southampton so he enjoys every moment he can with them. Paul is a huge fan of Moto GP so in his spare time he loves nothing more than to take his own motorbike for a spin!

Serves: 4   **Preparation time:** 45 mins   **Cooking time:** 3 hrs

Ingredients:
half a short side of pork belly (ask your butcher to score the belly, take off the rind and roll and tie it)
500 ml each of chicken and beef stock
500 ml good quality red wine
4 large carrots, peeled, cut into 2 cm dice
4 celery sticks, peeled, cut into 2 cm dice
300g baby shallots
2 large Maris Piper potatoes, peeled,

cut into 2 cm dice
50g freshly chopped parsley
3 Braeburn apples, diced with the skin on, core taken out
100g fresh thyme
3 cloves garlic, finely crushed
1 bay leaf
rock salt and white pepper
olive oil for frying
sherry vinegar to deglaze

Method:

To a medium sized heavy-based casserole dish add a little olive oil and get hot. Place the rolled belly into the pan and season with salt and pepper. Caramelise the belly all over until it is golden brown. Take the pork belly out of the pan and leave to one side.

Drain a little bit of the olive oil from the pan and add the vegetables, which will take on all the flavour of the pork belly. After about a minute, add the thyme, bay leaf and garlic and stir in. When the vegetables have taken on a nice colour, deglaze with the sherry vinegar, reduce the vinegar out then add the red wine and reduce to a sticky glaze. Add the pork belly back to the pan, pour over the stock, bring to a simmer, cover the dish and put into the oven at 140°C for about 3 hours or until you place a knife through the pork and it is meltingly tender.

When cooked, take off the heat and leave for 10 minutes to rest. Add the apples and fresh parsley and stir in well.

Leave for another 5 minutes and then serve in the middle of the table with some mashed potatoes and red cabbage.

A wonderful family sharing meal to all dig into around the table!

Shepherd's pie

Contributed by **Adam Byatt**

Supported by

About Adam: Adam graduated from Bournemouth College of Further Education in 1994. In 1996 he was in the national finals of the Young Chef of the Year and went on to be a judge in 2003/2004. He is a member of the Academy of Culinary Arts and partakes in the Princes Trust 'Chefs Adopt a School' programme. During his career he has worked at The Square, the two Michelin starred restaurant in Mayfair, along with Claridges and The Berkeley. Now 36, Adam has been Head Chef and proprietor of two very successful London restaurants and opened his third, Trinity, in 2006. In 2008 Trinity was named 'London Restaurant of the Year' at the AA Hospitality Awards and holds three AA rosettes. Apart from his successes at Trinity, Adam has appeared in numerous national and international television programmes and is a regular on the BBC's 'Saturday Kitchen'. Adam's sporting interests are fishing and walking his boxer, Roxy.

Serves: 6 healthy portions   **Cooking time:** 6 hrs, including preparation

Ingredients:
500g minced lamb belly
1 whole lamb shoulder (less knuckle)
2 onions, sliced
200 ml balsamic vinegar
1.2 litres brown chicken stock
2 stems of rosemary
2 whole garlic bulbs
2 large carrots, diced
600g turnips, diced

200g celeriac, diced
1 bay leaf
salt
vegetable oil

For the mash:
1.5 kg potatoes
250 ml milk
60g butter

Method:

Preheat the oven to 150°C.

Heat a large casserole pan with a splash of olive oil, season, and slowly brown off the lamb shoulder.

Once the shoulder is coloured, remove from the pan and add the minced lamb. Season with salt and pepper and cook over a high heat until well coloured.

Put all the root vegetables in the pan and brown them over a high heat. Once browned, remove and drain. You will need to retain these for the last assembly stage.

Remove the mince from the pan and add the onions to the same pan (you may need to add a touch more olive oil at this point). Brown the onions lightly and add the balsamic vinegar. Reduce by a third in volume.

Now place the coloured shoulder on top of the onions and add the two whole heads of garlic to the pan.

Add the stock to the pan at this stage.

Place a few thyme sprigs and a bay leaf in the pan and cover with a piece of parchment paper (not a lid).

Place into the preheated oven for 1¹/₂ hours, then spoon the juices over the meat and check that the shoulder meat is coming away from the bone with ease. The pot should need a

further 30 minutes to cook through completely.

Once cooked, remove the pan from the oven and allow to cool until you can handle the meat.

Remove the meat from the shoulder, fat and all, place into a bowl, add the browned off mince and onions and discard the bones and whole garlic.

Mix the meat thoroughly and place the mixture into a heat-proof casserole dish to finish the pie.

Place the pre-roasted vegetables on top of the meat mix and cover with the mashed potato.

Place the pie into a preheated oven at 200°C for a further 15 minutes to brown the potato.

Wafer thin apple tart with vanilla ice cream and honeycomb crisp

Contributed by **James Martin**   Supported by Vigilance Resources Ltd

About James: James's success can be attributed to his early love of food, which was nurtured at Castle Howard, where his father ran the catering and where James often helped out. At 16 he began his formal training at Scarborough Technical College, where he was Student of the Year three years running. Aged 22, he opened the Hotel and Bistro du Vin in Winchester as Head Chef and changed the menu every day. James's message about food has always been the same – he has been passionate about celebrating British food, using the best ingredients possible and creating simple, delicious recipes which are accessible to all. James has made a great impact since he appeared on television and has rarely been off screen since he began presenting BBC 1's hugely successful 'Saturday Kitchen'. More recently, James featured in 'The Real Italian Job'. The show, which saw James live his dream of competing in the exclusive Mille Miglia race in Italy in a vintage sports car, cemented his role as a car enthusiast and expert.

Serves: 4   **Preparation time:** 30 mins   **Cooking time:** 20 mins

Ingredients:
300g /11 oz puff pastry
6 Golden Delicious apples
225g /8 oz stewed Bramley apples
50g /2 oz melted butter
25g /1 oz caster sugar
flour for dusting
fresh mint
vanilla ice cream

For the honeycomb:
350g/13 oz caster sugar
2 tbsp liquid glucose
100 ml/3^1/$_4$ fl oz runny honey
100 ml/3^1/$_4$ fl oz water
1^1/$_2$ tsp bicarbonate of soda

Method:

Pre-heat oven to 200°C

Roll out the puff pastry thinly and dock the surface with a fork. Cut out four 8–9 inch discs. Place in the fridge to rest.

Peel and core the apples and cut in half. Slice thinly with a sharp knife. Remove the tarts from the fridge and place on a non-stick buttered baking tray. Lightly brush the edges of the tarts with melted butter and spread the stewed apples on the middle. Drizzle the top with the melted butter and sugar and bake for about 5–6 minutes, until golden brown.

While they are cooking, heat the sugar to a caramel and add the water to slacken and honey to taste. Allow to cool.

Remove the tarts from the oven and glaze with a little of the remaining butter. Place on the plates and serve with a spoonful of ice cream in the middle and the honeycomb crisp.

For the honeycomb you will need a heavy-based pan. Add the sugar, honey, glucose and water to the pan.

Place the pan on the heat and, using a sugar thermometer, bring to the boil and boil to 127°C (a light caramel).

Grease an oven tray while the sugar is boiling, remove the sugar from the heat and add the bicarb, stirring in quickly.

Working fast, pour the mixture onto the tray as it will start to bubble up straight away.

Leave to cool and when cold break into small pieces.

Place into a food processor and pulse until a powder, then, with a template, sprinkle over the top. Place into a warm oven for 2–3 minutes to allow to dissolve, then remove from the oven, allow to cool and remove from the tray. Allow to cool completely before serving.

Pineapple pavlova

Contributed by **Edmund Smith**

Supported by

SPINAL HOME CARE

About Edmund: From childhood Edmund was exposed to the hospitality industry, as his family owned The Maples, a very successful and well-known hotel in Dublin. He was always interested in the banqueting side of the business and used to help his father in the hotel. After graduating from Galway culinary college in Ireland, his preference was to work in a small restaurant, but later in his career he got a job at the Fairmont Hamilton Princess hotel in Bermuda, expecting to stay only a year. Then an opportunity came to run his own restaurant, Ascot's, in Hamilton, and 20 years on he now considers Bermuda his home! He acknowledges that his colleagues keep him on his toes and thinks the calibre of chefs in Bermuda is fantastic. His colleagues all get together the day before, giving ideas and suggestions to plan the next day's menu. In his spare time Edmund's sporting interests are golf and fishing.

Serves: 4   **Preparation time:** 25 mins   **Cooking time:** 45 mins

Ingredients:
1 baby pineapple
4 egg whites
225g sugar
1 tbsp vanilla essence
1 tbsp lemon juice
2 tbsp cornflour
1 pint heavy cream
caramel

Method:
Scoop out the inside of the pineapple and cook until soft with a little butter and sugar, then place back into the shell.

In a large bowl beat the egg whites until stiff, gradually adding the sugar. Beat until thick and glossy.

Gently fold in the vanilla essence, lemon juice and cornflour.

Pipe or spoon the mixture onto the pineapple half and bake for 45 minutes in a pre-heated oven at 300°F (150°C).

In a small bowl beat the heavy cream until stiff, add the caramel, pipe into a mould and serve.

Highcliff hot chocolate fondant

Contributed by **Clyde Hollett**   Supported by

About Clyde: Clyde's earliest memories are of being in the kitchen with his mum, and of having a clear sense of where his career path was headed. On leaving school he joined an apprentice scheme with a local hotel, with the added bonus of a day release college placement. This was the foundation of his career and he has never looked back! He then went from hotel kitchens to restaurant kitchens, where he learned not only the skills, but also the attitude and commitment that are necessary to succeed in the cheffing world. Clyde has had many successes, most recently when the Highcliff Grill was awarded and maintained two AA rosettes. In 2009 the Grill was awarded the Taste of Bournemouth Restaurant of the Year award, and in 2010 it won the Bournemouth Tourism Award for the Large/Medium Hotel of the Year. When he gets some spare time Clyde loves Formula One racing and keeps an eye on Premiership football.

Serves: 6-8   **Preparation time:** 30 mins   **Cooking time:** 8-10 mins

Ingredients:
250g 70% chocolate
250g unsalted butter
5 whole eggs

5 egg yolks
125g caster sugar
50g plain flour
6–8 $^1/_4$ pint pudding moulds

'This signature dish, which has featured for many years on the menu at the Highcliff Grill, is one of, if not the most, popular dessert on the menu, and, due to its sheer decadence, is always very well received by all who indulge.'

Method:

Before you start with the mixture, first prepare the moulds: soften a little unsalted butter and grease the moulds, then lightly dust the buttered moulds with coco powder, removing excess.

For the fondant mixture, over a bain-marie melt the butter and chocolate.

Whisk the sugar, whole eggs and egg yolks till doubled in size.

Gently fold in the melted chocolate and butter mixture, then fold in the flour and mix well.

Distribute the mixture between the prepared moulds and leave to set in a fridge for around 2 hours.

Bake in a pre-heated oven at 180°C for 8 minutes, then remove from the oven and turn the fondants out of the moulds.

Serve with fresh raspberries, crushed praline and white chocolate ice cream.

Chocolate and olive oil truffle with red pepper, raspberry jelly and Cornish sea salt

Contributed by **Simon Hulstone**   Supported by **C**ONTROL INDUCTION

About Simon: Simon's culinary career started early in his life and by his early teens he already held several World Junior titles. In 2003 he gained a Roux scholarship and in 2008 was named Knorr National Chef of the Year. Before moving to Torquay, Simon had been perfecting his culinary technique working in Michelin starred restaurants. Since taking over the helm as Head Chef at the Elephant, Simon has brought his extensive knowledge of traditional and world cuisine to Torbay, putting the English Riviera on the map. The Elephant now boasts a coveted Michelin star. Simon also flew the flag for Great Britain at the Bocuse d'Or in Lyon in 2011. Married to Katy with two young daughters, Tansy and Cicely, he shares with them a love of his adopted Devon and regularly does demonstrations locally. A keen traveller, Simon has dined at most of the best restaurants in the world. Outside work, Simon enjoys family life and rides and restores classic Lambretta scooters.

Serves: 4   **Preparation time:** 30 mins   **Resting time:** 6 hrs

For the truffle:
200 ml double cream
300 ml milk
500g dark chocolate
120 ml olive oil

For the jelly:
2–3 red peppers
400g raspberry purée
20 ml raspberry vinegar
200 ml water
100g sugar
7 leaves gelatine (soaked)

Method:

To make the truffle, bring the milk and cream to the boil, pour over the chocolate, then slowly mix in the olive oil. Allow to set for 6 hours before scooping. Serve with the red pepper jelly and sea salt.

For the jelly, roast and peel the peppers, then deseed. Place the vinegar, water, sugar, and raspberry purée into a pan and bring to the boil. Blitz the peppers and the liquid until smooth, then add the gelatine. Pass the mix and set in a tub.

Doppio cioccolato con pistacchio
(Double chocolate mousse with pistachios)

Contributed by **Gino D'Acampo**

About Gino: Born in Naples, Gino inherited his grandfather's love of cooking and went to the Luigi de Medici Catering College at the age of 15. He continued to develop his skills through the kitchens of restaurants in Europe, including a spell as Head Chef at Sylvester Stallone's Mambo King in Marbella (aged 19) before coming to England the following year. He has become a regular face on ITV's 'This Morning', has written four cookery books – the latest being *Pasta*, published in the Autumn of 2010 by Kyle Cathie – and has designed his own cookware range. Viewers took him to their hearts in 2009 when they voted him King of the Jungle in ITV's 'I'm A Celebrity, Get Me Out Of Here'. He also runs his own import company, Bonta' Italia.

Serves: 4 **Preparation time:** 20 mins plus 3 hrs chilling time

Ingredients:
150g dark chocolate (good quality and chopped)
100g white chocolate (good quality and chopped)
3 fresh eggs
2 tbsp caster sugar
2 tbsp amaretto liqueur
250 ml softly whipped cream
2 handfuls of crushed pistachio nuts

Method:

Melt the chocolate in a glass bowl over a pan with hot water (don't let the bowl touch the water). Once melted, set aside to cool, but not to harden.

Beat the eggs and sugar in a bowl until thick and pale. With the help of a metal spoon, fold the chocolate into the egg mixture. Add in the nuts and amaretto liqueur, mix well and then gently fold in the whipped cream.

Place the mixture into four separate dessert glasses (approx. 250 ml), refrigerate for 3 hours until set.

Just before serving, decorate with some crushed pistachio nuts on top.

Recipe cooked, plated and photographed by Cornwall College – St Austell.

Contributed by **Simon Haigh**   Supported by:

About Simon: Having worked in many of the country's finest country hotels, Simon embarked on his first Head Chef position at the age of 27 at Inverlochy Castle in Scotland. By the age of 30 he had gained a Michelin star, which he held for nearly eight years. Simon then moved to Mallory Court, where, in 2001, he achieved a star which he has held ever since. Outside work his family takes priority. Simon, his wife, Joanna, and their two sons, Joshua and Zack, try to do as much as they can together, and when he can Simon likes to play golf at Wilmslow Golf Club. He also has an avid interest in motorcycles and takes Joshua along to races, as his own father did when he was young, to encourage an interest in sports.

Salmon and caviar roulade en croute

Serves: 4   **Preparation time:** 1 hr

Ingredients:

6 slices smoked salmon
2 tbsp olive oil
100g crème fraîche

1 slice bread
1 pint double cream
chervil, chopped chives
60g caviar to garnish

Method:

Lay out smoked salmon on a sheet of clingfilm. Whisk ¹/₂ pint of cream to ribbon, and fold in the crème fraîche and chives. Put a spoonful of the mixture in the middle of a slice of salmon and roll into a tight tube. Freeze overnight. Cut the crusts off the bread, roll out to 2 mm thick and cut out circles with a small round cutter. Brush with olive oil and season with salt and pepper. Bake at 160°C (gas 6) for 10–15 minutes until golden. Allow to cool. Slice the salmon into ¹/₂ inch slices and place on the crouton. Garnish with caviar and chervil.

Bruschetta

Serves: 10   **Preparation time:** 20 mins

Ingredients:

1 small baguette
20 black olives
1 jar pesto
olive oil
1 tomato
salt and pepper
100g gruyère cheese

Method:

Slice the baguette lengthways down the middle. Place on a baking tray.

Slice the tomato and place on the tray next to the baguette. Drizzle with olive oil and season with salt and pepper. Bake in the oven at 160°C (gas 6) for 10 minutes. Remove from the oven, spread the bread with pesto and place the tomato on top. Grate the gruyère and place on top of the tomato.

Halve the olives and place them flat side down along the length of the bread. Return to the oven until the cheese has melted. Remove from the oven and allow to cool.

Cut into individual portions, using the olives as a guide.

Caramelised shallot and stilton croissants

Serves: 10   **Preparation time:** 1 hr

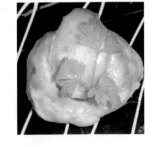

Ingredients:

100g puff pastry
1 tsp balsamic vinegar
1 diced shallot
1 egg
50g blue cheese
salt and pepper

Method:

Roll the pastry out to approx 2 mm thickness and cut into triangles $2^1/_2$ inches wide by 2 inches high.

Caramelise the shallot and mix with the cheese. Leave to cool.

Place a spoonful of the mixture in the middle of a pastry triangle, then roll up from the bottom so the pastry forms a tube. Pinch the ends of the tube in, and wrap them around until they join.

Place on a baking tray and brush with egg. Bake at 160°C (gas 6) for 12–15 minutes until golden.

... for Steven Duckworth and friends

Starter: Seared scallops with hot mustard shallot sauce
Main course: Sea bass with leek carbonara
Dessert: Bread and butter pudding

Contributed by **Gary Rhodes**   Supported by
British
Karate
Federation

About Gary: Revered chef, restaurateur and author Gary Rhodes has been at the forefront of the culinary world for over 30 years. He has achieved six Michelin stars and currently has eight restaurants spanning the globe, from the UK, to P&O cruise liners, to Dubai and Grenada. Gary has written 19 books, most recently *Gary Rhodes: 365,* and has appeared on numerous TV programmes, continuing to spread his love of 'Great British Classics' far and wide. A keen and avid Manchester United football supporter, Gary has even had the honour to cook for Sir Alex Ferguson and the team, which is one of the proudest moments of his career. Gary supports many charities and in 2006 was awarded an OBE for his services to the industry.

About Stephen: Stephen was a medical student at Guy's Hospital when he broke his neck in a freak rugby accident 29 years ago. Now 50, he and his four teenage boys all enjoy rugby. His claim to fame in the kitchen was working as a cook at a Little Chef restaurant aged 17. After his accident he qualified as a doctor and then gained a PhD in disability employment and was awarded an OBE for his services to disabled people. He currently runs a £100 million government contract helping long-term unemployed people get back to work. He also sits on the board of the Olympic Delivery Authority, the National Quality Board of the Health Service and the Disability Equality Delivery Board. Stephen's ideal guests for a dinner party would be JPR Williams, Rob Andrew and Jason Leonard.

Seared scallops with hot mustard shallot sauce

Serves: 4 **Preparation time:** as long as it take to make the mash

Cooking time: just minutes

Ingredients:

12 scallops, trimmed and cleaned of roe
225–350g mashed potatoes
50–85 ml single cream
hot mustard shallot sauce
1 tbsp cooking or olive oil
knob of butter
salt and pepper

For the sauce:

300 ml finely diced shallots or onions
small knob of butter
good twist of freshly ground pepper
50 ml red wine vinegar, preferably a thick, strong Cabernet Sauvignon variety
1 glass white wine
150 ml jus/gravy or alternative (it must have a good coating consistency)
1 tsp English mustard (not powder)
salt and pepper

Method:

Melt the butter in a small pan and add the chopped shallots or onions. Cook on a medium heat until they have started to take on a good golden brown colour – about 4–5 minutes.

Season with a twist of pepper and add the vinegar. Reduce the vinegar until almost dry, about 2–3 minutes.

Add the wine and continue to reduce, again until almost dry. Add the jus/gravy and bring to the simmer. Lightly simmer for 5–10 minutes and then add the mustard.

Season with salt and pepper, if needed, and taste. The sauce will now have a sharp, sweet flavour with a bite from the pepper and mustard.

The taste can be strengthened with a little more mustard.

Recipe method:

The mashed potatoes should be loosened with single cream; the consistency should be very soft but still holding its own weight. If, after adding the cream, the mash still seems to be too firm, add either more cream or milk. Check the seasoning.

Warm the mustard shallot sauce.

Heat a frying pan with the tablespoon of oil. Once hot, sit the scallops in the pan, making sure the maximum heat is maintained, which will ensure the scallops are searing. Season the scallops in the pan and, once a good, almost burnt, tinge has caught on the edges, add the knob of butter.

Leave for 30 seconds and turn the scallops over. They can now be cooked for a further 30 seconds to 1 minute.

To present the dish, either spoon or pipe the potatoes at the top of the plate. Spoon 2–3 tablespoons of sauce in front and sit three scallops on top.

Sea bass with leek carbonara

Serves: 4   **Preparation time:** approx. 15 mins   **Cooking time:** 15 mins

Ingredients:
4 x 175g (6 oz) sea bass fillets, skin on
salt and pepper
flour, for dusting
olive oil, for cooking
2 large knobs of butter

6 rashers of streaky bacon, cut into thin strips
3 leeks, cut into thick slices
150 ml (5 fl oz) double or whipping cream
2 generous tbsp grated Parmesan

Method:
Dry the sea bass on kitchen paper, season with salt and pepper and lightly dust the skin with flour. Heat the olive oil in a non-stick frying pan and add a large knob of butter. Once it begins to sizzle, place the fish in the pan skin side down. The fish may need to be gently pressed down with a fish slice because the skin tightens in the heat, slightly curving the fillets. Cook for 6–7 minutes to crisp and colour, then turn it and remove from the heat. The residual warmth in the pan will continue the cooking.

While the fish is frying, heat a large saucepan and add the bacon. Fry for a few minutes until golden, then spoon the strips on to a plate and pour off the excess fat in the pan. Melt the remaining butter and stir in the leeks with 3 tbsp water. Cover and steam for a few minutes until tender. Pour the cream over, simmer until lightly thickened, then spoon the parmesan cheese and bacon through the sauce. Serve with the sea bass on top.

Bread and butter pudding

Serves: 4 **Preparation time:** 30 mins **Cooking time:** 20–30 mins

Ingredients:

12 medium slices white bread, crusts cut off
50g unsalted butter, softened
1 vanilla pod or few drops of vanilla essence
400 ml double cream
400 ml milk
8 egg yolks
175g caster sugar, plus extra for the caramelised topping
25g sultanas
25g raisins

You will need 1 x 1.5–1.8 litre pudding dish/basin, buttered

Preheat the oven to 180°C/350°F/gas 4

Method:
Butter the bread. Split the vanilla pod, place in a saucepan with the cream and milk and bring to the boil. While it is heating, whisk together the egg yolks and caster sugar in a bowl. Allow the cream mix to cool a little, then strain onto the egg yolks, stirring all the time. You now have the custard.

Cut the bread into triangular quarters or halves and arrange in the dish in three layers, sprinkling the fruit between two layers and leaving the top clear.

Now pour over the warm custard, lightly pressing the bread to help it soak in, and leave it to stand for a least 20–30 minutes before cooking to ensure the bread absorbs all the custard.

The pudding can be prepared to this stage several hours in advance and cooked when needed.

Place the dish in a roasting tray three-quarters filled

with warm water and bake for 20–30 minutes until the pudding begins to set. Don't overcook it or the custard will scramble. Remove the pudding from the water bath, sprinkle it liberally with caster sugar and glaze under the grill on a medium heat or with a gas gun to a crunchy golden finish.

When glazing, the sugar dissolves and caramelises, and you may find that the corners of the bread begin to burn. This helps the flavour, giving a bittersweet taste that mellows when it is eaten with the rich custard, which seeps out of the wonderful bread sponge when you cut into it.

... for Geoff Holt and friends

Starter: Cornish crab with curry, apple and watercress
Main course: Roast chicken and Cornish chorizo pearl barley risotto
Dessert: Blackberry and apple crumble tart

Contributed by **Nathan Outlaw**   Supported by

About Nathan: Nathan is a 33-year-old chef, dad and restaurateur. He runs two successful restaurants at St Enodoc Hotel in Rock, Cornwall; Restaurant Nathan Outlaw and The Seafood and Grill Restaurant. Previously, his restaurant at the Marina Villa Hotel in Fowey received a Michelin star. This year Nathan has been firmly placed on the culinary map as Restaurant Nathan Outlaw was awarded two Michelin stars and voted Best Fish Restaurant by The Good Food Guide 2011. Nathan's huge passion for seafood stems from his time with Rick Stein at the Seafood Restaurant. He continues to champion local produce and in 2010 represented the South West on the BBC's 'Great British Menu'. His sporting interests are playing football and supporting Chelsea, boxing, basketball, sea fishing and surfing. The success of Nathan's restaurants means that he gets little time to pursue his hobbies, but he hopes to get back into them when his children are old enough to drag him out to join them.

About Geoff: Now in his 40s, Geoff has been married for 25 years to Elaine and they have a nine-year-old son, Timothy. An ex-professional yachtsman, Geoff still enjoys getting out on the water, and became the first tetraplegic to sail single-handed around Great Britain. He celebrated the 25th anniversary of his accident by sailing across the Atlantic. As a youngster he worked for six months in a Michelin starred restaurant. The taste for good food has stayed with him ever since, and his desire to replicate that same good food has been a source of constant irritation to his wife. In 2010 Geoff was awarded an MBE for 'Services to Disabled Sailing' and also won the prestigious 'Yachtsman of the Year' award. At sea he yearns for good food, especially when forced to rely on tinned food or, worse, dehydrated sachets. Geoff's ideal guests for a dinner party would be Sir Robin Knox-Johnson, Professor Richard Dawkins and Annie Lennox.

Cornish crab with curry, apple and watercress

Serves: 4 **Preparation time:** 15 mins

Ingredients for crab:
1 medium cooked brown crab or 500g
cooked crab meat
50 ml natural yoghurt
2 tsp chopped coriander
1 Granny Smith apple, peeled and
chopped or grated
watercress to garnish

For mayonnaise:
2 egg yolks
50 ml white wine vinegar
400 ml sunflower oil
$1/2$ tsp English mustard
2 tsp medium curry powder

Method:
Place the crab, yoghurt, coriander and
apple into a bowl and mix together.
For the mayonnaise, place the egg
yolks, vinegar, curry powder and
mustard into a bowl and whisk in the oil
slowly to emulsify to a mayonnaise.
Season to taste with a little salt. This
recipe will make more than required, but
it will keep for a week for other uses.

To serve:
Bind the crab mixture with some of the
mayonnaise to your personal taste. Take
4 starter plates and evenly portion up
the crab and sprinkle a few watercress
sprigs around the plate.

Roast chicken and Cornish chorizo pearl barley risotto

Serves: 4 **Preparation time:** 30 mins **Cooking time:** 20 mins

Ingredients:
1 medium organic chicken, roasted, legs picked down and breast meat diced

For pearl barley:
1 chopped white onion
200g button mushrooms
2 leeks, sliced finely
2 carrots, peeled and diced
2 cloves of garlic, chopped

150g pearl barley
100 ml white wine
50g unsalted butter
sunflower oil for cooking
600 ml chicken stock
100g mascarpone
a few drops of lemon juice
100g deli farm Cornish chorizo
100g cooked broccoli
2 tsp chopped parsley

Method:
Heat a large saucepan. Add a little oil and the butter. Melt butter then add the onion and leeks and sweat for 2 minutes. Add the barley and sweat for 2 more minutes. Add the white wine and reduce until all absorbed. Add the chicken stock, carrots, garlic and half the chorizo. Cook the mix until the barley is soft. Add water to top up if necessary. When the barley is cooked there should be little liquid left. Cool the mixture until required. To serve, sauté the mushrooms and chorizo in a little oil and drain. Reheat the barley mixture and add the mushrooms, chorizo, chicken, broccoli and parsley. Add the mascarpone, lemon juice and seasoning.

Blackberry and apple crumble tart

Preparation time: 40 mins   **Cooking time:** 40 mins

Ingredients for crumble:
100g unsalted butter
100g plain flour
100g Demerara sugar
100g caster sugar
100g ground almonds

For compôte: 2 bramley apples, peeled, cored and cut into 1 cm chunks
200g whole blackberries, washed

1 cinnamon stick
50g unsalted butter
50g caster sugar
50 ml apple juice or cider

For pastry: 2 medium eggs
225g unsalted butter, softened
1 tbsp caster sugar
275g plain flour and extra for dusting

Method:
For the compote, heat all the ingredients in a pan for 1 minute. Remove from the heat and cool. If too wet strain liquid off, reduce to syrup and add back. Once cool this is ready to use.

For the pastry, mix together the eggs and butter, then add sugar, then flour. Mix to a dough, wrap in clingfilm and chill for 1 hour.

Preheat oven to 190°C/gas 5. Grease tart case with melted butter. Roll out pastry and place in tin. Trim excess from sides of tin and rest in fridge for 1 hour (make individual tarts if you wish). Line pastry case with greaseproof and fill with baking beans. Bake for 15 minutes or until golden. Remove from oven and rest for 5 minutes before removing beans. Turn the oven to 200°C. Fill the tart with blackberry and apple mix and sprinkle crumble over the top.

Place in the hot oven for 10 minutes. Cool for 10 minutes before serving. Top with ice cream or clotted cream.

... for Owen Lowery and friends

Starter: Vichysoisse
Main course: Roast sea bass with Morteau sausage and clam chowder
Dessert: Chilled strawberry soup with summer berries and
mascarpone sorbet

Contributed by **Simon Gueller**   Supported by  Professional
Fitness & Education
EXCELLENCE THROUGH EDUCATION

About Simon: Simon and Rena Gueller opened their first restaurant in 1987. Yorkshire born and bred, Simon took over the once-famous Box Tree in 2004, carefully reinstating it to its former glory as one of the UK's top restaurants; just four months later he earned a Michelin star. Simon is a keen sportsman and has always put his health and fitness first. He used to do a lot of running and occasionally plays football with his team from the restaurant. In 2002 Simon had a back injury that led to surgery and since his recovery has taken up mountain biking, which has less impact on his spine. Based in the heart of the Yorkshire moors, Simon can often be seen mountain biking. He and Rena also go two or three times week to spin/rpm classes and like to take their children on long walks on the moors.

About Owen: Owen suffered spinal injuries in 1987 at the age of 18 in a judo accident, having previously won numerous national judo titles, including the Men's British Closed in 1986 when 17 years of age. Owen feels the years have flown by since then. After his accident he spent two years in hospital, and the following years were spent studying, socialising and watching football, as well as studying for a PhD relating to war poetry. Owen loves reading and writing poetry in general, with his preferences in food including single malts! Owen's ideal guests for a dinner party would be Graeme Souness, Ian Botham and Seamus Heaney.

Vichysoisse

Serves: 6   **Preparation time:** 20 mins   **Cooking time:** 30 mins

Ingredients:
750g leeks, very finely sliced
350g onions, peeled and finely sliced
350g potatoes, peeled and very finely sliced

900 ml fish stock (boiling)
900 ml chicken stock (boiling)
200 ml cream
100g butter

Method:
1. Sweat the onions & leeks in the butter until they are soft but without colour.
2. Add the sliced potato and the boiling stocks and cook over a fast heat for 10 minutes.
3. Add the cream and cook for a further 2 minutes. Liquidise, then pass through a fine sieve. Season to taste.

Roast sea bass with Morteau sausage and clam chowder

Serves: 6 **Preparation time:** 1¹/₂ hrs **Cooking time:** 5–7 mins

Ingredients:
2 shallots
pinch cracked white pepper
250 ml white wine
250 ml Noilly Prat
500 ml fish stock
660 ml double cream
100g baby spinach
24 palourde clams
6 bay leaves

100g each finely chopped celery, fennel, carrot, onion and leek
200g piece Morteau sausage
200g chopped potatoes (Maris Piper)
50g chopped parsley
pinch cayenne pepper
1 lemon
Maldon sea salt
6 bass portions

Method:
For the velouté, sweat the shallots and pepper without colour. Add the white wine and reduce by half. Add the Noilly and reduce by half, add fish stock and reduce to syrup, add cream, bring to the boil. Remove from heat, blitz with a hand blender and pass through a fine sieve. Chill till needed.

Slice 24 thin slices of the Morteau, lay out on a tray and oven cook at 170°C until golden brown. While still hot fold slices over a round implement. Dice the rest of the Morteau, fry in clarified butter until coloured and put aside.

Cook the bass in vegetable oil skin side down for 1 minute on a high heat. Transfer to the oven for 3–4 minutes until cooked. Meanwhile, sweat the spinach in a water and butter emulsion.

Prepare the chowder by adding the fried Morteau to the chopped vegetables and velouté. Boil and reduce slightly. Season with salt, lemon juice and cayenne pepper to taste. Steam the clams in a covered pan with olive oil, bay leaf and a little water until they open (1–2 minutes).

Cook the chopped vegetables in butter till tender (5–7 minutes). Cook the finely chopped potatoes in milk with salt, pepper and bay leaf until soft. Chill.

To serve, place a ring of spinach in the middle of the bowl and arrange the velouté with the vegetables around it. Arrange the clams and Morteau tuilles over the chowder. Place the bass on the spinach. Arrange herbs such as micro-celery and parsley over the chowder. Finish with good quality olive oil.

Chilled strawberry soup with summer berries and mascarpone sorbet

Serves: 6 **Preparation time:** 15 mins **Cooking time:** 40 mins
For sorbet: Preparation time: 10 mins **Freezing time:** 4 hrs

Ingredients:
1 kg strawberries
125g caster sugar
450g mascarpone

575 ml stock syrup (equal parts sugar and water)
55 ml lemon juice (4 tbsp)

Method:
Hull and slice the strawberries and gently mix with the sugar. Leave in a warm place for 1 hour.

Pour mixture into a piece of muslin and tie and leave to strain over a bowl in the fridge overnight.

Blend the syrup and mascarpone thoroughly and place in an ice-cream machine. When almost frozen add lemon juice. Continue churning until frozen. Place in freezer (use within 3 days). (If an ice-cream machine is not available, simply serve a tablespoon of mascarpone.)

Pour the strawberry soup into a bowl, garnish with fresh raspberries, strawberries and blueberries and just before serving top with mascarpone sorbet (or mascarpone).

Above right: *Chilled strawberry soup with summer berries and mascarpone sorbet.*
Above left: *Roast sea bass with Morteau sausage and clam chowder.*

... for Moray Cook and friends

Starter: Crab meat ravioli
Main course: Beef Wellington with spring vegetables
Dessert: Chocolate fondant with rum-marinated berries

Contributed by **Lars Windfuhr**   Supported by

About Lars: Lars commenced his career with Hyatt International in May 1999 as a Demi Chef de Partie for Hyatt Regency Cologne, and in the past ten years he has worked at Grand Hyatt Amman in Jordan and at Hyatt Regency La Manga in Spain. In September 2009, Lars was recognised for his management skills, innovative cuisine and passion for creating 'the best' and was awarded with a promotion to Executive Chef at Hyatt Regency London – The Churchill. Lars says: 'Cooking is my passion and I am very proud to now be part of the team at Hyatt Regency London – The Churchill and to be in London amongst some of the most exciting and dynamic chefs in the world.' In his spare time, which is quite rare, Lars enjoys trekking, swimming and snorkelling.

About Moray: Moray sustained his injury in 1999 whilst on holiday celebrating the completion of his MSc in Chemistry and French from Bristol University. After 13 months' rehabilitation at the National Spinal Injuries Centre, Stoke Mandeville, Moray was discharged to live independently in Bedfordshire with the help of PAs. He completed a year-long Postgraduate Diploma in Psychology at Nottingham University in 2004/05 and in 2010 was finishing a three-year doctorate in Counselling Psychology at City University, London. He hopes to continue working with people with spinal cord injuries after qualifying. Moray's ideal dinner party guests would be Vic Reeves, Frankie Boyle and Louis Theroux.

Crab-meat ravioli

Serves: 4   **Preparation time:** 1 hr   **Cooking time:** 3–5 mins

Ingredients, pasta:
250g '00' pasta flour, plus extra for dusting
1 egg yolk
3 eggs
2 tbsp water
2 tbsp olive oil

Crab meat filling:
400g blanched crab meat
100 ml double cream
100 ml concentrated crab stock
1 tsp finely chopped fresh tarragon
1 free-range egg + 1 free-range egg yolk

pinch cayenne pepper
squeeze lemon juice

Crab cream sauce:
200 ml crab stock
150 ml double cream

Spinach:
500g washed spinach
1 tbsp butter
cherry tomato
olive oil

fried leek juliennes

Method:
Place all of the pasta ingredients into a food processor. Pulse until the mixture resembles fine breadcrumbs. Tip onto a floured work surface and knead for about 5 minutes, or until the mixture comes together to form a smooth dough. Roll into a ball, wrap in clingfilm and chill in the fridge for 15 minutes. Feed the piece of dough through a pasta machine, starting at the lowest setting; change the setting to the next-thickest setting, flour it again and feed the pasta sheet through again, as before. Repeat 3–4 more times, flouring the machine and changing the setting down each time. Once the pasta sheet has reached the ideal thickness, lay out on a floured tray and set aside. You should have two equal-sized rectangles.

For the crab filling, place all the crab meat into a food processor and blend to a paste. While blending the mixture, slowly pour in the double cream in a continuous stream, followed by the stock, and blend until smooth. Chill down and let rest in the fridge for a while, then spoon the mixture into a piping bag.

To make the ravioli, pipe four small mounds of the filling onto one pasta sheet at equal distances apart and not too close to the edge of the pasta sheet. Using a pastry brush, moisten the edges around each individual pile of filling with water, leaving a 3 cm gap. Lay a second sheet of pasta over the first. Cut through both pasta sheets between the piles of filling to form 4 ravioli. Carefully press down the moistened edges around the filling and pinch the edges to seal. Bring a large pan of water to the boil. Add the ravioli and cook for 3–5 minutes, or until the ravioli is al dente. Remove with a slotted spoon and set aside until served.

For the crab cream, bring the stock to the boil and then stir in the cream until well combined. Keep simmering for 10 minutes over a medium heat to reduce.

Wash the cherry tomatoes, drizzle with some olive oil and roast at 180°C for about 4 minutes.

Heat up a large enough pot, add the butter and sauté the spinach leaves for 2–3 minutes.

Arrange the spinach in a pre-warmed plate, top with the ravioli, pour over a ladleful of the crab sauce, then top each plate with cherry tomatoes and the fried leek juliennes.

Beef Wellington with spring vegetables

Serves: 4   **Preparation time:** 45 mins   **Cooking time:** 10 mins

Ingredients:
0.75 kg middle cut beef fillet, trimmed
$1/2$ bunch thyme, finely chopped
sea salt and freshly ground black pepper

For duxelles:
50g butter

1 clove garlic, finely chopped
250g button mushrooms, finely chopped

Wellington:
500g/1lb 2oz block puff pastry
1 egg, lightly beaten, to seal the pastry
melted butter, to glaze

Method:
Preheat the oven to 250°C. Season the beef with the thyme, sea salt and pepper. Heat a pan and sear each side of the beef quickly. Set aside to rest.

For the duxelles, sweat the butter, garlic and mushrooms in a pan over a low heat until all the moisture evaporates. Remove from heat and cool to room temperature.

Lightly dust a sheet of baking paper with flour. Roll the puff pastry so it is a little wider than the beef, and the beef can be completely rolled in pastry. Spread the duxelle mixture evenly over the half of the pastry closest to you.

Place the beef on top of the mushroom mix and roll the beef up in the pastry, leaving a slight overlap of 3 cm. Brush this with beaten egg and seal. Trim the ends of the pastry so they are flush with the beef.

Place the beef Wellington on a sheet of baking paper cut to size, lightly brush with melted butter and refrigerate for 30 minutes.

Cook the beef Wellington in the preheated oven for 10 minutes or until dark golden in colour.

Serve with spring vegetables.

Above: *Beef Wellington with spring vegetables.*
Right: *Chocolate fondant with rum-marinated berries.*

Chocolate fondant with rum-marinated berries

Serves: 4 **Preparation time:** 1 hr **Cooking time:** 10–12 mins

Ingredients:
50g melted butter, for brushing
cocoa powder, for dusting
200g good quality dark chocolate,
chopped into small pieces
200g butter, in small pieces
200g golden caster sugar
4 eggs and 4 yolks

200g plain flour

200g mixed berries (raspberries,
blackberries, strawberries, blueberries)
100 ml rum
100g sugar

vanilla ice cream

Method:
Prepare the moulds by brushing the melted butter all over the inside of the pudding moulds and adding a good spoonful of cocoa powder into each one. Tip each mould so that the cocoa powder completely coats the butter. Tap any excess cocoa back into the jar.

Slowly melt the chocolate and butter together, then remove the bowl from the heat and stir until smooth; let it sit for about 10 minutes.

In a separate bowl whisk the eggs and yolks together with the sugar until thick; sift the flour into the eggs, then beat together.

Pour the melted chocolate into the egg mixture in three lots, beating well between each addition, until all the chocolate is added and the mixture is completely combined.

Divide the mixture between the moulds and chill for at least 20 minutes. You can prepare this cake batter the day before.

Heat oven to 200°C. Place the fondants on a baking tray and then cook for 10–12 minutes until the tops have formed a crust and they are starting to come away from the sides of their moulds. Remove from the oven, then leave to sit for 1 minute before turning out.

Wash and clean the berries, dry them on a kitchen cloth and marinate with sugar and rum.

... for Julie Sawyer and friends

Main course: Pea and chervil risotto with pea shoots and goats' cheese
Dessert: Vanilla crème brûlée

Contributed by **Tom Aikens**   Supported by INDICATER
bite-size hospitality management software

About Tom: Tom has been cooking since the age of 16 and with his identical twin brother, Rob, studied at Norwich City College Hotel School. Following this, he secured his first job at the Mirabelle restaurant in Eastbourne. He then moved to London and worked with the likes of Pierre Koffmann and Richard Neat, followed by a period working in France. After returning to London he worked at various restaurants and then spent two years working in the private sector for Lord Lloyd Webber and the Bamford family. In April 2003, Tom Aikens Restaurant was opened in Chelsea and soon earned a Michelin star. Tom's second restaurant, Tom's Kitchen, serving home-style brasserie cooking, opened in 2006, followed by Tom's Kitchen at Somerset House in 2010. Tom loves cycling and has entered numerous races in France. He also enjoys running and in 2010 ran the Marathon des Sables in the Sahara Desert for charity.

About Julie: Julie became tetraplegic following a motorcycle accident 13 years ago. After spending ten months in Stoke Mandeville, she trained and worked as a Drug & Alcohol Counsellor with young people before going on to do a degree in Criminology & Social Policy. She is currently on the verge of completing a PhD in Citizenship, Consumption and the Environment. Becoming a Buddhist in 1997, home cooking and good food have become a genuine passion for her, especially as vegetarians often have limited choices in restaurants. Julie's ideal dinner party guests would be Paul McCartney, Benjamin Zephaniah and Victoria Wood.

Pea and chervil risotto with pea shoots and goats' cheese

Serves: 4–6   **Preparation time:** 20 mins   **Cooking time:** 18 mins

Ingredients for pea stock:
600g fresh or frozen peas
1.2 litre vegetable stock or boiling water
6g caster sugar
2g salt
20g chervil
10g fresh mint

For risotto:
250g risotto rice
800 ml pea stock

200g cooked fresh peas
100g butter
100 ml olive oil
2g salt
50g grated parmesan
4 banana shallots, peeled and diced finely
250 ml white wine
80g crème fraîche
12g chopped chervil
50g soft goats' cheese

Method:
Boil the vegetable stock with the salt and sugar, add the peas and cook for 2–3 minutes till soft. Purée in a blender with the chervil and mint, then chill. Pass this liquid through a fine sieve into a bowl over iced water. Heat a pan on a low heat. Add the olive oil and sweat the shallots with no colour. Add the rice and cook for 2 minutes, stirring all the time. Add the white wine and cook till absorbed (it will take a minute or so). Add the pea stock little by little, stirring every minute or so. It will take around 12–14 minutes till the rice is almost cooked. Add the fresh peas and when it is almost ready add the crème fraîche, parmesan and chervil and re-season. Rest for a minute then serve, garnished with pea shoots and goats' cheese.

Pea and chervil risotto with pea shoots and goats' cheese.

Vanilla crème brûlée

Serves: 4 **Preparation time:** 10 mins **Cooking time:** 45 mins

Ingredients:
375g cream
125g milk
4 egg yolks

75g sugar
1 vanilla pod, split and scraped
1 tsp vanilla essence

Method:
Whisk the egg yolks with the sugar and the vanilla bean until pale.

Add the milk and cream and essence.

Leave this for 1 hour to infuse, whisking now and again.

Pass through a fine sieve and place into a shallow ceramic dish – no more than 2 cm deep.

Place into the oven at 90°C for approximately 45 minutes to 1 hour until it is jelly-like, set.

When this is ready, place into the fridge to chill for 45 minutes to 1 hour.

Sprinkle with caster sugar, then blow-torch till golden.

... for Steve Helley and friends

Starter: Spring pea soup with caramelised scallops, crushed peas & smoked bacon crisps

Main course: Pan-roasted sea bass fillet with Spanish potato salad and rocket leaf salad

Contributed by **Brett Camborne-Paynter**

Supported by

About Brett: As a young boy growing up in Milton Keynes Brett realised his love for cooking and food in his mum's kitchen, where he would quiz her about cooking methods and ingredients. Once qualified as a chef, Brett made a beeline for London, where he worked with Jean Christophe Novelli at the Four Seasons, later moving to The Waldorf, The Ivy, Le Caprice and J Sheekey to gain even more experience! In 2007, at the age of 31, Brett became Chef Proprietor of Austell's restaurant in Cornwall, which gained 2 AA rosettes and a Michelin Guide listing within six months of opening. Brett is keen to use fresh, locally sourced ingredients for his varied menus. In his spare time Brett enjoys spending time with his family cycling, swimming and exploring the Cornish countryside!

About Steve: Steve is 50 years old and lives in Torpoint, Cornwall, with his wife, Mary, and two children, Katie and Jack. He has been living with a spinal cord injury for 36 years after a trampoline accident whilst at school. He loves plain, traditional, wholesome food and eating out. He worked for 25 years in local government and now works voluntarily as a psychotherapist in GP surgeries. He likes to travel and watch football and sometimes goes to the Emirates Stadium to see Arsenal play and attends most of Plymouth Argyle's home games. He also enjoys the cinema and theatre, along with driving, and can often be found taxiing his children around. Stephen's ideal dinner party guests would be Ian Wright, Tony Adams and Arsene Wenger.

Spring pea soup with caramelised scallops, crushed peas and smoked bacon crisps

Serves: 4 **Preparation time:** 45 mins **Cooking time:** 5 mins

Ingredients:
8 hand-dived scallops, cleaned
8 slices smoked pancetta bacon
400g frozen petit pois
40g butter

For the pea soup:
280g onions, finely sliced
38g celeriac, 1 cm dice
15g leeks, washed and shredded

63g potato, 1 cm dice
8g garlic, crushed
$^1/_2$ pkt butter
$2^1/_2$ g sea salt
375 ml vegetable stock
375 ml milk
600g frozen peas
120g white wine vinegar
10g sugar

Method:
For the soup, sweat onions, celery, leeks, potato and garlic in the butter, with no colour, lid on, for 30 minutes. Add the liquids, bring to the boil, add the frozen peas, blend and chill on ice. Reduce the vinegar and sugar to 45g then add to soup. Reheat when needed to serve.

For the purée, bring to the boil 2 litres of water, cook the peas for 1 minute, drain thoroughly and blend with seasoning and butter for 30 seconds to a coarse purée. (Make in advance if you like and warm in a microwave.)

Bake the bacon slices on a non-stick tray at 200°C for 6–7 minutes or until golden brown and crispy.

For the scallops, heat a little olive oil in a non-stick pan over a medium heat. Season them with salt and freshly ground black pepper, place in the pan sliced side down and cook until golden-brown, about 1–2 minutes. Turn them over, reduce the heat and cook for 1–3 minutes until just done (don't overcook!).

Remove scallops from the pan, place on a tray lined with kitchen paper and squeeze over a little lemon juice.

To finish, warm 4 tbsp of the purée in the microwave for 40 seconds, divide between 4 warmed bowls, then heat the soup and add to the bowls. Place 2 scallops onto the purée and finish by laying 2 slices of bacon on top.

Enjoy!

Spring pea soup with caramelised scallops, crushed peas and smoked bacon crisps.

Pan-roasted sea bass with Spanish potato salad and rocket leaf salad.

Pan-roasted sea bass with Spanish potato salad and rocket leaf salad

Serves: 4   **Preparation time:** 40 mins   **Cooking time:** 10 mins

Ingredients:
4 x 200g fillets of sea bass (scaled and boned)
100g wild rocket salad

For the balsamic dressing:
6 tbsp extra virgin olive oil
2 tbsp balsamic vinegar
1 level tbsp clear honey

For the Spanish potato salad:
150 ml olive oil
3 large banana shallots, sliced

1 clove garlic, crushed
1 tsp smoked paprika
1 tsp cumin powder
1 tsp sweet paprika
450g chorizo sausage, sliced
3 red peppers, roasted and diced
100g Lingham's sweet chilli sauce
$^1/_2$ bn coriander chopped
200g cherry tomatoes, quartered
500g new potatoes, cooked and sliced

Method:
For the potato salad, lightly fry the shallots, garlic and spices for 5 minutes in the olive oil. Add the chorizo and cook for a further 15 minutes. Away from the heat add the peppers and other ingredients. Leave for 10 minutes to infuse.

For the dressing, simply place the ingredients in a bowl and mix together.

For the sea bass, lightly dust the skin side (not the flesh side) in seasoned plain flour. Shake off any excess. Heat a frying pan to high and add olive oil. Put the fillets in the pan, one by one, skin side down. To stop the fillets curling press down with your fingers and/or a spatula to keep them flat. Do not move the fillets around or moisture will get under the skin and they will start to steam instead of fry. The fillets will start to cook at the edges of the top fleshy side. When there is a translucent strip of uncooked fish down the middle (the fillet will be cooked at the edges) turn them over for no more than 30 seconds just to seal the last remaining uncooked fish. Put the fillets to one side, off the heat.

To serve, warm 4 plates, pile the warmed potato salad in the centre, top with the cooked bass fillets and then with rocket leaves dressed with the balsamic dressing. Serve immediately.

... for Tom Doughty and friends

Starter: Beetroot and coconut samosa
Main course: Masala nu roast gos
Dessert: Allé bellé – Goan coconut pancakes

Contributed by **Cyrus Todiwala**   Supported by

About Cyrus: An expert in Pan-Indian cuisine, Cyrus has won countless awards for culinary excellence, and is co-owner with his wife, Pervin, of Café Spice Namasté in London. Does Cyrus ever long to slow down? Not likely. Since leaving his native Bombay in the early '90s to set up his restaurant in London, Cyrus has had boundless energy and creates refined Parsi and Goan-inspired dishes in his own kitchens when not writing cookbooks (he has published three), appearing on TV (he's a regular on both 'Market Kitchen' and 'Saturday Kitchen') and at food festivals, and donating time to charity. Cyrus has always championed local British produce, environmentally friendly practices and staff training. Cyrus's main sporting interest is now cricket, and in the past table tennis and long-distance running.

About Tom: Tom is 54. He lives life independently and to the full following a motorcycle accident at the age of 17. He has travelled most of the world, including a visit to Kolkata in 2007 to play guitar with an Indian lap-guitar master. He cycles using a hand cycle and takes his dog, Frank, with him for three miles each day. He works hard as a musician and to date has released three albums. He performs throughout the UK and abroad. Two of his gigs for 2011 will be on the Main Stage at The Bridgewater Hall with a capacity of 2,300 and at The Singapore Guitar Show. Tom is perhaps the only solo tetraplegic guitarist in the world. After 35 years using a wheelchair he feels optimistic about the next 35! Tom's ideal guests for a dinner party would be Ronnie Wood, Brian May and Mark Knopfler.

Beetroot and coconut samosa

Serves: 12–15 **Preparation time:** 45 + 45 mins **Cooking time:** 5–8 mins

Ingredients:
500g beetroot
½ tsp mustard seeds
½ tsp cumin seeds
¼ tsp hing (asafoetida)
6–8 fresh curry leaves
2 medium green chillis
6–8 tbsp grated coconut
1 pkt samosa (spring roll) pastry
oil for frying
2 tbsp oil for sautéing
salt
4–5 tbsp flour
2–3 tbsp water

'Whilst many feel that the simple beetroot is a root vegetable fit only for boiling and salads, we Indians do much with it. Known in Hindi as Chukunder, there are some fabulous preparations one can do with it. Healthy, full of iron and immensely tasty, the beetroot has much regard in the culinary history of Indian cuisine. In Britain try to get hold of Cheltenham beets – they are amazing. They are not the usual round shape but more longish with a flavour to match the best root vegetables anywhere. We use Cheltenham beets in our samosas.'

Method:
Wash the beetroots well and trim off the leaves (these cook very well as a bhaji). Finely shred the curry leaves, mince the green chillis and set aside.

Boil the beets or steam in a pressure cooker. Pressure cooking will retain the beetroots' natural goodness, and they cook faster and stay deeper red, too. Cool, peel and cut into ½ cm x ½ cm dice.

In a wok or kadhai heat the two tablespoons of oil until a haze forms over it and add the mustard seeds.

Allow them to splutter (to prevent them flying out of the pan you may cover with a mesh). Reduce the heat a little. Do not allow to burn, but as soon as the seeds have almost stopped crackling, add the cumin seeds and as soon as they change colour add the curry leaves and the green chilli.

Sauté for 1 or 2 minutes at most, then add the asafoetida and, almost immediately, the grated coconut.

Keep stirring from the bottom up once the coconut is added, as it will tend to stick at the bottom of the pan – a flat wooden spatula is the best tool for this.

Once the coconut is dry and almost toasted, add the beetroot and sauté for a few minutes until the dice feel dry to the touch. Check the seasoning, remove and cool.

For the samosas you will need to buy frozen spring roll pastry in (oriental supermarkets sell it in 8 or 9 inch square sheets). One packet is more than sufficient.

Thaw the pack intact without opening.

Take the whole pile of sheets out of the packing and place on a chopping board.

Place an upside down side plate on the pile so that only the square edges are visible. Cut around the plate to make a pile of pastry rounds, then cut the pile into half to form even semicircles.

Now peel off two thin sheets at a time and place under a plate to prevent drying.

Make a thick, gluey paste from the flour and water.

Form cones from each of the double pastry semicircles, fill with the beetroot stuffing, fold over and seal again with the paste to form triangles. (First fold over ⅓ of the sheet onto the larger portion, apply some paste and then fold the ⅔ side over to form a perfect cone – practice makes perfect!)

Heat the oil once the batch is ready and fry at roughly 180°C on all sides.

Serve with a fresh green chutney or ketchup.

Masala nu roast gos

Serves: 4 **Preparation time:** 25–30 mins **Cooking time:** 1.5–2 hrs overall

Ingredients:
4 lamb shanks (400g each, roast trimmed)
50g ginger
50g garlic
1 tsp cumin
1 tbsp coriander seeds
2 1-in pieces cinnamon or cassia bark
3–4 green cardamoms
2–3 cloves
3–4 peppercorns
3 medium sized chopped onions
200g chopped tomatoes
2–3 tbsp sunflower oil
1 tsp salt (and then to taste)
1 dozen or so small potatoes

Method:
Trim the shanks to suit as for roasting. Roast the cumin and coriander on a low heat until they change colour slightly and cool. In a blender grind together the ginger, garlic and the roasted cumin and coriander to a fine paste with only as much water as is necessary to keep the condiments moist. Peel the potatoes, remove any spots, wash and keep them soaked in water. In a large casserole big enough to take the shanks of lamb add the oil and heat until a light haze forms on the surface. Reduce the heat a little, add the lamb and brown well on all sides until the meat is well sealed. Remove the lamb from the casserole and add the whole spices. Sauté on a low heat until the cloves swell a bit, then deglaze the casserole with a little water to release the residue from the lamb stuck at the base. Scrape with a wooden spatula until the base is clean and add the chopped onions. Continue cooking until the liquid evaporates, sauté the onions until soft and add the ground masala. Add some water to the container to release any stuck masala and add this to the pan too. Continue cooking for 5–6 minutes and put the lamb back into the casserole. Coat it well with the masala, check seasoning and add salt as desired. Lower the heat a bit, cover the pan tightly and continue cooking the lamb.

At this stage, if your casserole is an ovenable type, put it covered into the oven at approximately 150°C. After about 15 minutes remove from the oven, turn the meat and put it back into the oven.

If cooking it on the cooker top turn the meat after 10 minutes or so and also check to see that the contents are not burning. If necessary add some water or stock to loosen the contents at the bottom of the pan.

In another 15 minutes or so the lamb should be approximately half cooked.

Now add the chopped tomatoes and potatoes and if necessary some water or stock, cover and continue cooking for another 10–15 minutes.

When the lamb is almost cooked the muscles at the shin will have retracted and the lamb will feel soft to the touch. If in doubt, insert a thin skewer or roasting fork and check that the fluid released is running clear.

When the lamb is done remove it onto a tray and also remove any gravy stuck to it.

Remove the potatoes and set these aside. Check the gravy and, if necessary, add enough liquid to have a pouring consistency.

Serve the lamb hot with the gravy and the potatoes or serve it later by slicing it when cold. To serve hot, heat the gravy and the lamb with the potatoes, covered, in a hot oven for 10 minutes and serve with the gravy poured on top. A little fresh chopped coriander adds a touch of magic to the gravy. Best served with chunks of deep fried parboiled potato and steamed rice.

This Parsee style roasted joint of lamb may be sliced and served cold as a sandwich filler, served hot with the gravy, with boiled rice or a light cumin pulao. This style of marinating is very adaptable, and the simplicity of it all makes it suitable for most meats.

Allé bellé – Goan coconut pancakes

Serves: 6 **Preparation time:** 1 hr

Ingredients for six pancakes:
10–12 tbsp grated coconut (if using desiccated, soak in water before use)
1 tbsp sultanas
75g palm molasses (If not available, use cane molasses, or jaggery, as we call it. Do not use liquid.)
¼ tsp ground cardamom
¼ tsp ground nutmeg

Ingredients for batter:
1 tbsp unsalted butter
200g plain flour
150 ml coconut milk
1 tbsp caster sugar
pinch salt
a few drops of vanilla extract
a pinch of grated lemon rind

'This traditional Goan sweet is thoroughly enjoyable with vanilla ice cream when served warmed and lightly buttered. Can also be served with cream. However, in Goa it is often eaten on its own. Roasted cashew nuts can also be added for additional flavour.'

Method:
For the filling, mix all the ingredients together.

For the batter, melt the butter and mix it into the flour, along with the salt and sugar. Add the coconut milk and a little water and mix well to a smooth pouring consistency. Add the vanilla and the lemon zest. Check the consistency and proceed to make your pancakes as you would normally. Stuff and roll whilst the pancakes are warm. Brush with butter and heat prior to serving either on their own or with cream, custard or vanilla ice cream.

... for David Follett and friends

Starter: Whipped cheese mousse with mixed salad and candied walnuts
Main course: Trio of lamb, beef & pork fillets
Dessert: Flamed baked Alaska with strawberry coulis

Contributed by **Mike Monahan**   Supported by **restaurant** MAGAZINE

About Mike: In a widespread and varied career, Mike started out as a Commis Chef at the Hotel Piccadilly in Manchester, followed by a spell at Gravetye Manor under Michael Quinn. A Head Chef position at Linden Hall Hotel, Morpeth, was combined with lecturing. After working in Bahrain, Mike became Executive Sous Chef at the Inn on the Park in London. An Executive Chef position at Billesley Manor was then achieved, followed by a similar position at La Quinta Club at La Manga, Spain. Mike then worked in both Portugal and Spain, finishing with a period in Portugal at the Penina Golf and Resort hotel in the Algarve. In 1994 he joined P&O Cruises and is now Culinary Manager for Carnival UK. In the past he has worked on most of the company's ships. Since 2010 he has been responsible for 10 vessels, including the recruitment of chefs and all other aspects of the catering. Mike enjoys golf and working out at the gym, and for further relaxation he enjoys reading cookery books.

About David: David is a 20-year-old C6/7 tetraplegic. Two weeks after his 18th birthday he was having a kick about with a football at the beach when he went out into the road to retrieve the ball and was hit by a car. Following rehabilitation at the spinal unit at Salisbury District Hospital, he returned to his home town of Exeter. He was a keen football player prior to his accident and still enjoys watching it. Sport is David's passion, and he now plays wheelchair badminton and hopes to go on to coach the sport. He feels that he is a typical lad who likes takeaways and cooks basic recipes, but he comes from a foodie family and enjoys some great food with them. David's ideal dinner party guests would be Pele, Stephen Hawking and Steven Gerrard.

Whipped cheese mousse with mixed salad and candied walnuts

Serves: 4 **Preparation time:** 15 mins **Cooking time:** 10 mins

Ingredients:
200g Gorgonzola cheese
40 ml milk
40g mascarpone cheese

40g radicchio lettuce
80g chicory/Belgian endive
80g curly endive/frizzy

40g walnut halves
20g caster sugar
50g watercress leaves
1 each sliced red and green apples
1 celery stick
25 ml lemon juice
2 ciabatta or french stick roundels, toasted

Method:
Melt the Gorgonzola cheese into some warmed milk, add mascarpone cheese and beat into a soft mousse, then place in a piping bag.

To make candied walnuts, boil the walnuts in stock syrup and allow to dry overnight on silicon paper and then deep fry until crisp. Allow to cool.

Oven toast the ciabatta bread – serve 3 pieces per portion.

Prepare the endive leaves and arrange as below.

Slice celery into thin batons.

Slice apples as seen below and dip into lemon water to retain colour.

Trio of lamb, beef and pork fillets

Serves: 4 **Preparation time:** 45 mins **Cooking time:** 15 mins

Ingredients:
300g lamb cannons
300g beef fillet medallion
300g pork fillet roundels

Garnish:
500g fondant potatoes
500g pumpkin purée

100g broad beans
500g courgettes

Madeira sauce:
100g chopped shallots
50g butter
250 ml Madeira wine
300 ml veal jus lié

Method:
Wrap all the meats in cling wrap to form round cylindrical shapes.

Wrap both the lamb cannons and pork fillets in outer foil and roast in a hot oven, then, once cooked to a pink/medium degree, remove from the oven and remove both the foil and cling wrap and sear on broiler top to obtain colour on the outside of the meats before slicing.

The beef fillet can be cut into roundels whilst still in the cling wrap, then carefully remove the band of cling wrap from each steak after cooking and sear the edges to obtain colour.

For the Madeira sauce, melt the butter and sauté the shallots, add the Madeira and reduce to a syrup.

Add the ready-made veal jus lié and simmer for 30 minutes.

Strain and monté with soft butter to enrich the sauce and season to taste.

Flamed baked Alaska with strawberry coulis

Serves: 4 **Preparation time:** 45 mins **Cooking time:** 20 mins

For the sponge disc bases:
10g flour
15g sugar
2 eggs
vanilla essence
60 ml brandy (for soaking sponge)
400 ml vanilla ice cream
150 ml flambé brandy for flambé
40g dark chocolate (run-out on plate)

For the meringue:
4 egg whites
250g caster sugar

For the strawberry coulis:
160g strawberries
50g icing sugar
fresh lemon juice

Method:
Bake the sponge mix and cut out discs. Soak the sponge discs with brandy.

Scoop the vanilla ice cream onto the sponge discs.

Place egg whites in a bowl, whisk until they forms peaks and add sugar a spoonful at a time till all sugar is absorbed and it looks glossy.

Pipe the meringue around the ice cream, ensuring that it is completely sealed, then hold in freezer until required.

Use a blow torch to colour the meringue before serving.

For the coulis, heat the strawberries in a large pan until they start to break down, add sugar and cook until it has dissolved.

Transfer the coulis mixture to a food processor and blend until it

is smooth.

Decorate plate with strawberry coulis, etc., as shown, using a piped chocolate run-out on plate to maintain shape Flambé with warm brandy at the table.

... for John McCafferty and friends

Starter: Shrimps with whisky and girolles
Main course: Beef brisket in Guinness and prune juice
Dessert: Lemon syllabub

Contributed by **Marco Pierre White**   Supported by  Unilever Food Solutions

About Marco: As a little boy growing up in Leeds, Marco found inspiration and joy in nature and what it can supply. Amazingly, he earned his three Michelin stars without ever having visited France, the home of fine cuisine, let alone worked there. Marco had already realised that Mother Nature is the true artist, and that his role was to show off her ingredients to their best. Born in 1961, he trained to be a chef with the likes of Albert Roux, Nico Ladenis, Pierre Koffmann and Raymond Blanc. At 24 Marco became Head Chef and joint owner of Harvey's and at the age of 33 became the first British chef, and the youngest chef ever, to achieve three Michelin stars with a kitchen staff that included Gordon Ramsay and Heston Blumenthal. Marco, who now works as ambassador for KNORR, also has extensive business interests across the world. His sporting interests are shooting and fishing.

About John: John is a 29-year-old C5/6 tetraplegic. He damaged his spine on holiday while swimming in the sea off a Greek island. It was near the end of his holiday so he feels he didn't miss much! Following this he spent two years in a care home after rehab at the RNOH Stanmore and has been living independently in a bungalow for the last five years with a live-in PA/carer. He coaches football part time for the Tottenham Hotspur Foundation, is on the committee at Community Focus – a local accessible arts centre – and studies photography at Middlesex University. John's ideal guests for a dinner party would be Gary Mabbutt, Eddy Temple-Morris and Chuck Close.

Shrimps with whisky and girolles

Serves: 4   **Preparation time:** 10 mins   **Cooking time:** 10 mins

Ingredients:
2 handfuls girolle mushrooms
extra virgin olive oil
15–20 large shrimps
a splash of whisky
a splash of Knorr concentrated chicken
stock
a knob of unsalted butter
fresh herbs of choice to garnish
Maldon sea salt
black pepper

Method:
Finely slice the girolles, keeping the shape of the mushrooms.

In a large frying pan, heat a generous amount of olive oil and fry the shrimps for a minute or so until they are golden and caramelised on one side. Turn the shrimps over and fry the other side and add the mushrooms to the pan.

Continue to fry for another minute or so. Throw in the whisky, toss the shrimps and mushrooms and stand back while the alcohol ignites and burns away.

Add the stock and the butter. Now stir until the shrimps are golden brown and glazed in butteriness.

Scatter over the fresh herbs and salt and pepper and serve from the pan.

Beef brisket in Guinness and prune juice

Serves: 4   **Preparation time:** 10–15 mins   **Cooking time:** 4$^1/_4$ hrs

Ingredients:
2 onions, halved
2 cloves garlic, peeled
extra virgin olive oil
500 ml prune juice

550 ml Guinness
200 ml water
Knorr beef stock cube
1.3kg beef brisket, trimmed and cut into
8 pieces

Method:
Preheat the oven to 140°C/gas 1. Pulp the onions and garlic in a food

processor (or use a hand-held stick blender) until it is almost a purée. Heat 1–2 tablespoons of olive oil in a casserole, add the onion/garlic pulp and fry over a low heat, stirring frequently, until the purée melts and smells delicious. It will take 5–6 minutes to cook, but don't brown it.

Remove the casserole from the heat and add the prune juice, Guinness, water and stock cube. Set aside.

In a large, heavy-based frying pan, heat some olive oil – be generous with it – and then brown the beef for a minute or two on each side, turning only once. Remove the beef pieces from the pan, patting them dry with kitchen paper.

Add the beef to the casserole and cook in the oven for 4 hours, or until the meat is delicately tender.

Lemon syllabub

Serves: 4   **Preparation time:** 20 mins   **Cooking time:** 20 mins

Ingredients:
2 lemons
80g icing sugar
500 ml double cream
3 tbsp Limoncello liqueur

For the lemon syrup:
80g caster sugar
juice of 3 lemons
40 ml water

Method:

In a saucepan make the syrup by combining the caster sugar with the water and bring to the boil. Just before it starts to colour, add the lemon juice. Boil for a few minutes until it has thickened and remove from the heat (remember, the syrup will be a lot thicker when it cools). Peel the lemon so that you end up with long matchsticks of lemon zest and then, with a sharp knife, slice away the pith. Blanch the zest by putting it into a saucepan of water, bring to the boil, count to 10 and remove from the heat. Refresh the zest by draining it in a colander and immediately running under cold water for a few seconds. Repeat this process twice. Making the syllabub will take just a minute or two. Combine the icing sugar and cream and whip to a thick ribbon consistency, being careful not to over-whisk (unless you want to end up with cheese). Fold in the strips of lemon and chilled lemon syrup and finish by drizzling over the Limoncello.

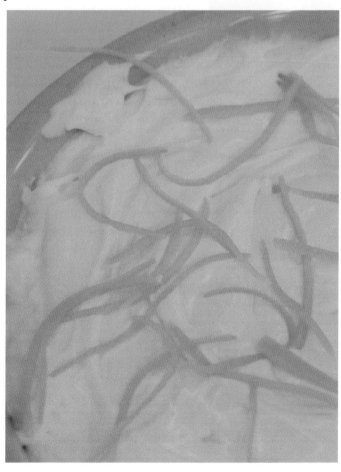

... for Glenn Bilbrough and friends

Starter: Scallop sashimi with watermelon and feta dressing
Main course: Grilled wagyu beef on horseradish creamed potato
Dessert: Spiced berry, maple syrup and vanilla risotto

Contributed by **Peter Gordon**   Supported by

Photo:Jonathan Gregson

About Peter: Chef, restaurateur and writer Peter Gordon is the 'godfather' of fusion cuisine, which he first introduced at the award-winning Sugar Club and continues to explore at his London restaurants The Providores & Tapa Room and Kopapa. Peter pushes the boundaries of where one national cuisine starts and another stops. 'Fusion can create the most stimulating meal you'll ever eat,' he says. 'It's fun and it's playful. It's simply one of many cuisines, and it happily sits amongst them like a magpie, borrowing from them all.' Peter has written six cook books, the most recent being *Fusion: A Culinary Journey*, and contributed to another dozen. Peter is widely recognised as a strong promoter of the food industry in both his native New Zealand and the UK, where he uses his culinary skills to raise money for numerous charities, as well as culinary competitions that promote excellence amongst younger chefs and waiters. Peter's annual charity event for leukaemia in the UK, 'Who's Cooking Dinner?', has raised more than £3.7 million over 13 years. Peter was awarded an ONZM in the 2009 New Year's Honours List for services to the food industry. Peter's only form of sporting activity or decent exercise of late has been walking, but he has promised himself he'll start cycling again.

About Glenn: Glenn is 44 years old and a C6 tetraplegic. He was injured skiing in Austria on Christmas Eve 2007. A big skier prior to his accident, skiing six to eight weeks a year, he was back on the slopes three days after his discharge from hospital thanks to the Back-Up Trust. He has since skied in Sweden and still spends Christmas in Austria. Glenn is currently in the process of returning to work as an Air Traffic Project Specialist. He has been with his wife, Rebekah, for 10 years. His ideal dinner party guests would be Franz Klammer, Valentino Rossi and Chuck Yeager.

Scallop sashimi with watermelon & feta dressing

Serves: 4 **Preparation time:** 5 mins

Ingredients:
4 large scallops with coral attached
(or 6–8 smaller scallops)
¼ small watermelon
30 ml (2 tbsp) soy sauce

30 ml (2 tbsp) lemon juice
50g feta, cut into small dice
15 ml (1 tbsp) extra virgin olive oil
cress to garnish
1 lemon, cut into wedges

Method:
Clean the scallops, removing the tough muscle, which sits opposite the coral and looks like white gristle, if it's still attached. Remove the coral and cut roughly into dice – you'll need 1 tablespoon worth in total. Slice each scallop into three discs of even thickness, place on kitchen paper on a chilled plate, cover with plastic wrap and place in the fridge.

Cut the rind and any white pith from the watermelon. Cut into 12 slices or wedges, removing as many pips as you can. Don't butcher the melon in the process, though – a few pips won't hurt anyone.

Place in the fridge to chill down for 20 minutes.

Mix the soy and lemon juice together in a small bowl and add the scallop slices. Leave to marinate for just 20 seconds, then remove them

and drain.

To serve, lay a slice of watermelon on each plate, lay a scallop disc on top and repeat this until you have three slices of watermelon and the scallops are used up. Scatter the feta and coral on top. Sprinkle with a little flaky sea salt, drizzle with the olive oil, sprinkle with the cress and place a lemon wedge on each plate. Eat immediately.

Grilled wagyu beef on horseradish creamed potato with soy buttered shimeji & pickled enoki mushrooms

'Any good quality beef will work with this recipe – you don't need to use wagyu. Best cuts would be sirloin, fillet, rib-eye or even rare cooked onglet. Serve this with buttered cabbage and green beans or a crisp green salad.'

Serves: 4   **Preparation time:** 20 mins   **Cooking time:** 30 mins

Ingredients:
150g shimeji mushrooms
100g enoki mushrooms
100g butter
50 ml soy sauce
80 ml rice vinegar (or any white vinegar)
2 tbsp caster sugar
800g floury potatoes
200 ml cream
2 tbsp freshly grated horseradish, or use horseradish from a jar (more or less to taste)
15 ml (1 tbsp) olive oil or rapeseed oil
4 x 180g steaks, trimmed of sinew, at room temperature
cress or something pretty to garnish

Method:
Cut the base from both types of mushroom then separate each mushroom from the clump – keeping them separate. Heat up a frying-pan, add half the butter and cook until it begins to turn golden. Add the shimeji and cook over a moderate heat, stirring, until they begin to wilt. Add 40 ml of the soy sauce, put a lid on, and turn the heat quite low. Leave them to cook/steam for 5 minutes, shaking the pan from time to time, and keep warm.

Put the vinegar and sugar into a pan with 150 ml water and 1 teaspoon flaky salt. Bring to the boil, add the enoki and take off the heat. Leave to cool in the liquid, then decant into a bowl.

Peel the potatoes and halve them, then boil in lightly salted water until cooked. Drain the potato into a colander and put the pan back on the heat with the remaining butter and the cream. Bring to the boil, return the potato to the pan and mash it all together with the horseradish. Season with salt and keep covered and warm.

Heat up a heavy-based pan or skillet over a moderate to high heat.

Rub the oil over the wagyu steaks and season generously with black pepper and salt. When the pan is hot, place the steaks in and cook until well coloured,

then turn them over and cook the same on the other side. Sear all sides of the wagyu so it's brown and caramelised. Take from the heat, but keep warm and covered. Rest for 5 minutes. Don't overcook them or all their lovely flavour will be lost.

To serve, divide the mash between four warmed plates. Slice the steaks in half and rest on the mash, tuck the shimeji in and then place some of the drained enoki on top.

Add the wagyu cooking juices, the remaining soy sauce and a little of the enoki pickling liquid to the shimeji pan juices, and use this to sauce the dish. Garnish with cress.

Recipes © Peter Gordon, from *Fusion: A Culinary Journey*, published by Jacqui Small. Photography: Jean Cazals.

Spiced berry, maple syrup and vanilla risotto

Serves: 4 **Preparation time:** 5 mins **Cooking time:** 20 mins

Ingredients:

200g (1 cup) risotto or paella rice
60g unsalted butter
½ vanilla bean, split lengthways
4 green cardamoms, crushed lightly
with the side of a knife
4 cm stick cinnamon

2 cloves
100g mascarpone
80 ml maple syrup
2 tbsp icing sugar
120g raspberries
120g strawberries, hulled and halved
120g blueberries

Method:

Rinse the rice for 10 seconds in a sieve under warm running water.

  Place in a medium-sized pot and add 600 ml water, the butter, vanilla and spices. Bring to the boil, then simmer for 15 minutes with a tight-fitting lid on.

Check to see if the rice is cooked, and when it's almost ready mix in the mascarpone, maple syrup and sugar, then gently stir in the berries. Put the lid back on, take off the heat and leave for 5 minutes in a warm place. Gently stir it again and it's ready.

'This simple dessert will be as tasty as the fruit you use. Berries in summer, stone fruit towards autumn, diced pears and apple in winter. Try using different spices, too – grated fresh ginger, star anise, allspice, etc.'

Petit fours

Contributed by **Ruth Hinks**

Supported by

About Ruth: Born in South Africa, Ruth has over 26 years' experience. She trained at the Silwood Kitchen Cooking School in South Africa, specialising in pastry. After graduating, Ruth travelled to the UK and secured her first job at the London Hilton. Other jobs followed in Sydney and Scotland, followed by a spell at the Windsor Hotel in Melbourne, where she joined the Australian Culinary Olympics Team. During 2000 Ruth worked for renowned chef Albert Roux. In 2002 she returned to Australia and was named Australian Pastry Chef of the Year and in 2004 won a Gold, Silver and Bronze in the Culinary Olympics. In the same year Ruth met David Hinks, and in 2005 they married and relocated to Peeblesshire, where Ruth became Head Pastry Chef at the Sheraton Grand Hotel in Edinburgh. In 2008 Ruth launched Cocoa Black Chocolate & Pastry School and she continues to compete, winning 'best chocolates' in the 2010 UK Chocolate Masters. Ruth enjoys swimming, tennis and hockey.

Chocolate financiers filled with chocolate cream

Preparation time: 24 hrs

Ingredients:
90g icing sugar
35g almond flour
25g all-purpose flour
10g cocoa powder
1g baking powder
90g egg whites
4g rum
50g brown butter

200g chocolate chips

For the Manjari crémeux:
base crème anglaise
200g cream
200g milk
80g yolks
40g sugar
95g Manjari chocolate

Method:
Prepare brown butter with the butter and set aside to cool.

Combine and sift all the dry ingredients.

Add the egg whites to the dry ingredients until fully mixed, then slowly add the browned butter.

Add the rum and chocolate chips and stir gently until mixed well.

For the crémeux Manjari, prepare an anglaise with the milk, cream, yolks and sugar heated to 85°C.

Pour the hot crème anglaise over the chocolate and mix until homogenous.

Let crystallise in the fridge for 24 hours until ready to use.

Macaroons

Preparation time: 20 mins   **Cooking time:** 20 mins

For the chocolate macaroons:
220g icing sugar
10g cocoa powder
120g ground almonds
100g egg whites
25g caster sugar

For the plain macaroons:
230g icing sugar
120g ground almonds
100g egg whites
25g caster sugar
food colours

Method:
Preheat the oven to 150°C.

For the chocolate macaroons, sift the icing sugar, cocoa powder and almonds into a small bowl and set aside.

Put the egg whites in another bowl and beat with an electric beater until they form firm peaks. Add the sugar little by little, beating until the mixture is smooth and shiny.

Sprinkle in the dry ingredients and delicately mix with a spatula until smooth and shiny.

Spoon the mix into a piping bag, form small macaroons on baking paper and bake on two trays for 15–20 minutes.

Stick together with chocolate ganache.

Make up a plain macaroon mix with the ingredients above, omitting the cocoa powder, and add food colouring as required.

Chocolate tarts

Preparation time: 40 mins   **Cooking time:** 15 mins

For the chocolate sweet pastry:
135g all-purpose flour
15g cocoa powder
60g butter
60g icing sugar
40g yolks
10g eggs

For the chocolate filling:
100g dark chocolate
zest of an orange
85g double cream

Method:
For the pastry, combine butter, sugar and mix a bit.

Add eggs and yolks, then flour, cocoa powder and salt, mixing until the dough has just come together.

Roll out nice and thin, line your tart shells and bake until cooked, about 8–10 minutes at 180°C.

For the filling, bring the cream and orange zest to the boil and pour over the chocolate. Allow to stand for a few minutes and blend well.

Coffee truffles

Preparation time: 12 hours (rest overnight)

Ingredients:
160g cream
20g liquid glucose
20g sugar

350g chocolate
20g butter
10g coffee essence

Method:
Bring the cream, glucose and sugar to the boil. Pour it over the chocolate, coffee essence and butter.

Mix well and allow to sit overnight.

Scoop the truffles and roll them in melted tempered chocolate. Dust with silver chocolate shimmer powder.

Appendices

About Hospitality Action

For over 170 years Hospitality Action, the Hospitality Industry Benevolent Organisation, has been at the forefront of the industry, providing specialised support to all who work, or have worked, within hospitality in the UK and who find themselves in crisis.

Hospitality Action offers vital assistance to those who need it most, people such as Annie Giles-Quinn, who worked for the hospitality industry for nearly 30 years before turning to the charity.

After separating from her husband it was left to Annie to financially support her two children. As a single mother times were tough but Annie gained confidence in herself and the family pulled together.

Then tragedy struck. Annie was diagnosed with breast cancer on two separate occasions. With her children dependent upon her the impact on family life was hard. If coping with cancer hadn't been enough, Annie's sight began to deteriorate. She was forced to leave her job and in 2007 was registered blind.

Depressed, isolated and lonely, she turned to Hospitality Action for help.

The charity were able to provide Annie with special speech activated software so she could use her computer again. Although only a small change this had a huge effect on the family's life.

Annie can once again carry out tasks such as online shopping so reducing her dependency on her children. Thanks to email she can now stay in touch with her friends, preventing those creeping feelings of loneliness.

Hospitality Action facts
- The charity helps people experiencing a range of adverse circumstances, from serious illness through to poverty, bereavement and domestic violence.

- In 2010 alone Hospitality Action spent £394,666 supporting 1,497 people in need. 41% of people helped were suffering from life changing illness and 23% were suffering from poverty.

- 74% of those Hospitality Action supports are under the age of 60.

- There are numerous ways to get involved with the charity all year round such as attending events, becoming a member or volunteering.

Mr & Mrs Smart with their car port.

Another example of who the charity supports is Mr & Mrs Smart. Around 100,000 people in the UK suffer from multiple sclerosis. Morag Smart is just one.

For a decade Morag and her husband, Iain, worked as successful lodge managers on the Isle of Skye. Their welcoming and kind-hearted approach to lodge life ensured their guests returned year after year. Gradually, however, Morag's health began to decline and she was diagnosed with MS. The news hit Morag and Iain hard, and both were forced to leave their jobs; Morag due to her failing health and Iain so he could care for her. As Morag's disease rendered her unable to walk she became dependent on Iain for nearly everything. Getting in and out of the couple's car took longer and longer, and the severe Skye weather conditions forced Morag to cancel many medical appointments. She simply could not get to the hospital, causing her condition to worsen.

Morag was then sadly diagnosed with breast cancer; she required surgery followed by medication, which was not without its side effects.

It was on the recommendation of Morag's Occupational Therapist that a car port be built to shelter her from the harsh winds and rain as she prepared to travel. With no means to fund the car port themselves Hospitality Action stepped in, ensuring Morag never had to cancel another hospital visit. The charity was also able to assist with vital bathroom modifications, enabling Morag to regain some of her independence.

Family Members

Hospitality Action also supports those who have worked within the industry but are now retired. The Family Members Scheme is a great way for our beneficiaries to make new friends and catch up at regular lunches. They also receive a free bi-monthly newsletter with interesting features and relevant news

Family Members attending a lunch. From left to right: Mrs Ryder and Mrs Lees.

stories, as well as being visited in their own homes by a friendly volunteer where required.

The Volunteer Visitors provide someone to talk to in confidence as well as friendship for this often forgotten about group of individuals.

Part of Hospitality Action

The Ark Foundation

The hospitality industry can be a demanding place to work, with many employees exposed to drink and drugs. The Ark Foundation, part of Hospitality Action, helps tackle the problems of the excessive effects of these substances via educational seminars. These seminars are carried out by experienced industry professionals who have fallen victim to substance abuse. Since 2001 The Ark has spoken to 60,000 catering students offering advice on how to avoid peer pressure and cope with their heavy workplace demands.

Many thanks for purchasing this cookbook, enjoy experimenting with the delicious recipes safe in the knowledge that the money donated to Hospitality Action will go a long way towards helping those in need.

For more information and ways to support the charity please contact:

Hospitality Action
62 Britton Street, London, EC1M 5UY
Tel: 020 3004 5500
Fax: 020 7253 2094
Web: www.hospitalityaction.org.uk
Email: info@hospitalityaction.org.uk

Registered Charity No: 1101083

About REGAIN

R E G A I N

The Trust for Sports Tetraplegics

what is tetraplegia?

Tetraplegia, sometimes referred to as quadriplegia, is the result of a severe spinal cord injury, which affects both sensation and mobility because messages to the brain have become interrupted resulting in paralysis. A tetraplegic individual will be unable to walk and have limited reach and dexterity because use of the arms is also impaired.

Advances in medical treatment and rehabilitation mean that the issue for tetraplegics and their families is no longer one of life expectancy, but of aspirations and expectation of life. The challenge is for more and sophisticated technology which will enable them to become fully integrated members of society, for tetraplegics to regain their independence and quality of life, and for the community to regain their many and varied talents.

what does REGAIN do?

REGAIN is the only charitable organisation in the UK dedicated solely to improving the independence of men and women who have become tetraplegic as a result of a sports injury.

The charity does this by providing financial help to purchase a wide range of specialist equipment, including voice-activated computers; environmental control systems for the home; sports wheelchairs; hand cycles and adaptations to cars, bikes and even planes. And also by encouraging tetraplegics to take part in sporting activities again. Additionally, REGAIN aims to provide professional and emotional support by directing tetraplegics to the relevant professionals for counselling, legal or other professional help or through the time and support of volunteer helpers and other tetraplegics.

who has been helped?

three of the hundreds of tetraplegics who have been helped by REGAIN (Regainers)

James Price was 21 years old when he broke his neck in a diving accident while on holiday in Majorca. Now 26, James was selected for the Great Britain Wheelchair Rugby squad just six months after REGAIN bought him a custom-built sports wheelchair. "Wheelchair rugby is the key to fulfilling my goal of making the most of my second chance in life. Without Regain's help I wouldn't have got this far,' said James.

At the time of his accident Edward Gaffey was only 16 years old and a successful young athlete. Because of his severe paralysis, for the past 21 years Edward has had to rely on friends and family to push him everywhere. What he needed, but was unable to afford, was a specially adapted electric wheelchair. REGAIN was able to do that. "The wheelchair has completely changed my life," says Edward.

John Roney broke his neck in a rugby match when he was 22 years old. Now aged 36, John requested a lightweight wheelchair which he felt would give him added independence. Following REGAIN's purchase of the wheelchair for him, John says his dream has been realised. He can now get in and out of his car without having to rely upon others. This has enabled him to get out and about much more and he is now the chairman of a newly formed charity promoting freedom for the physically challenged. "The independence REGAIN has given me has been invaluable," he says.

who needs help?

some of the tetraplegics who have requested support from REGAIN

A 17-year-old who broke his neck in a rugby accident is in desperate need of a standing powered wheelchair with chin control for a C2 ventilator dependent patient. He would also like a laptop computer with voice controls.

A 38-year-old man from Clerkenwell, London, who sustained a C5/C6 level injury as the result of a cycling accident in France, has requested financial assistance towards the purchase of an exercise machine costing £700.

A 22-year-old from Kent, who was body surfing in Australia when he broke his neck at level C5 in 2003, would like a pair of e-motion wheels costing approximately £4,000.

A rugby scrum accident last year left a 44-year-old man paralysed with a C3/4 injury. He needs a secondhand wheelchair and a page turner to enable him to read independently.

statistics
In the UK some two people every day will become paralysed as the result of a spinal injury. Many of them are young people taking part in sporting activities.

REGAIN has assisted more than 200 tetraplegics (Regainers) by purchasing specialist equipment. Regainers currently registered with the charity were injured as a result of participation in the following sports:

Diving	76
Rugby	69
Motocross etc.	20
Gymnastics	12
Swimming	7
Riding	3
Indoor football	3
Motor racing	3
Handgliding	2
Skiing	2
Water-skiing	1
Skydiving	1
Others	4

the history of REGAIN
In 1993 a charity called the Trevor Jones Trust was formed by former Royal Navy helicopter pilot Trevor Jones, who broke his neck in a skiing accident in 1988. The aim was to help people with similar injuries to regain their independence. The charity was renamed REGAIN, the Trust for Sports Tetraplegics, in 1995 to more accurately reflect its work when Trevor left to pursue his own ambitions, including sailing round the world.

Since then the trustees and supporters of REGAIN have worked hard to improve the quality of life for British sports tetraplegics by purchasing specialist equipment and by practically encouraging men and women to take up sport after their injury. The charity purchases specialist equipment for tetraplegics; organises sports taster days; provides hand cycles to enable tetraplegics to take up cycling and funds many wheelchair rugby players and other sports people, as well as providing practical advice.

The charity's Patrons include Sir Richard Branson, Dame Tanni Grey-Thompson DBE and Jason Leonard MBE. Lord Ivar Mountbatten is Chairman of REGAIN's Trustees.

how much money does REGAIN need to raise?
The charity receives at least two new applications a month for assistance and makes grants to tetraplegics as and when funds become available. The charity raises on average between £100,000–200,000 per year to support its work. There are always more tetraplegics in need of funds to buy specialist equipment than REGAIN can ever hope to support.

Without support REGAIN cannot provide the equipment and help so many severely paralysed men and women need. Raising funds for REGAIN makes a real difference to the lives of many tetraplegics.

The charity relies entirely upon funds raised by supporters and grant-making organisations to support its work.

REGAIN
78 Shirburn Road, Watlington
Oxon OX9 5BZ
Telephone: 01491 613980
e-mail:
enquiries@regainsportscharity.com
website: www.regainsportscharity.com

Registered Charity No. 1030693

When undertaking research for this book into the needs of other disabled people eating out or eating at home, I did not want to focus on the question of access, as the Disability Discrimination Act (DDA), which now forms part of the Equality Act, has been in force for some time. However, many of the returned questionnaires mentioned problems either inside restaurants or in accessing them. The hospitality industry is legally bound under the Equality Act to provide 'reasonable access', and while many proprietors act in good faith, others appear not to be doing so. It is therefore hoped that those establishments to which 'reasonable access' may not have been provided, or where an access audit has yet to be carried out, can benefit from the information in this book. Even in those establishments already compliant with the DDA, there may still be some areas where improvements can be made, as mentioned in my introduction and on the Feedback page. Further advice, if needed, can be obtained from the likes of Tourism for All and the Centre for Accessible Environments. In respect of the recipes and meals contained in the book, most were given in good faith by the supporting chefs before any guidance was given. Others were given in the hope that they would meet the needs of those with limited dexterity. As a result, I appreciate that, as some recipes and meals do not tick all the boxes, so to speak, in respect of being disability friendly, this book cannot claim to be a panacea for all. However, I hope the recipes are still enjoyable to cook and eat, and that the responses to my questionnaire, printed here, give further guidance to chefs and others for the future. Any difficulties faced by disabled people eating out or at home that perhaps are not covered on the feedback page or elsewhere can be relayed via the website **www.davidcroft.info**. Likewise, any needs, tastes, desires or ideas for improvements in the future in respect of making food for disabled people easier to eat can be relayed via the same website. Each response received will go into a draw to win a complimentary night's break for two at the Thistle Marble Arch, London, inclusive of dinner and breakfast.

• A lot of places are not wheelchair friendly nor have an accessible toilet. – **KT**

• Although not a big meat eater, I would sometimes like to order a steak but avoid doing so as I don't like having to have it cut up. It would be less embarrassing if staff cut things up in the kitchen before serving. – **ST**

• A choice of cutlery would make life easier. – **CM**

• As a C4 complete tetraplegic it is table settings and table heights that sometimes make eating out difficult, as I have to sit away from the table, as my chair will not fit underneath it, which means that I don't feel part of the party. Better planning in restaurants in where you are placed when having pre-booked a table and informed them you are in a wheelchair would help. – **CH**

• I avoid food that I can't cut up independently, but I can physically manage most dishes. Table heights and lips under tables can often cause problems. – **TD**

• Position of different items on the table and food easily explained to someone with a visual impairment would help. – **Mr C**

• Meat for me needs to be off the bone and seafood out of its shell. Food arriving nice and hot also helps, as it takes extra time for my PA to feed me while also eating. – **Mr N**

• Menus need to be read out to me, and sealed sauce, butter and milk containers can sometimes cause problems. – **BD**

• Contrasting tablecloths and place settings needed, e.g. light mat on dark cloth and vice versa. – **Mrs B**

• Unless I specifically constrain my menu choices to either pasta or risotto, the vast majority of foods either involve large vegetables or fish (with bones in) or meat that needs cutting up. Tables you can actually get your legs underneath would help, e.g. no cross band, therefore you don't have to stretch all the time or sit sideways. – **JS**

• A choice of cutlery would be good, and an exact list of ingredients for each dish would help. – **AK**

• Having been diabetic for 62 years I find restaurants do not serve plain food without sauces or dressings. – **JC**

• I have weak and painful hands and arms. I dread food that is difficult to cut and pick up. I like the trendy fashion of large plates. Small plates overflowing with food are embarrassing. Straight-sided glasses are difficult, as I can't grip them, and top-heavy stemmed glasses are likely to tip over. – **WT**

• Time between courses usually too quick. – **Mrs C**

• Serving food in bowls or on plates with sides so that a spoon or fork can scoop up food would help me. Having at least two or three choices from the menu, which are in mouth-sized pieces, would also help. Salad could also be chopped up so it provides mouth-sized potions. – **SP**

• Large-print menus would help, and an exact list of ingredients for each dish would also help. – **DP**

• As a vegetarian and having a disabled relative who is not vegetarian, going out for a meal often results in us being offered risotto. While we both enjoy risotto it would be nice to have other options. – **HT**

• I love seafood but I often have to choose a scallop dish. Something different and more creative without bones in and in mouth-sized pieces would make for a more enjoyable meal. – **DP**

First, I would like to thank all the chefs who responded so positively to my initial letter, and, while it may have taken some time for me to give them further details of the project, my apologies go to those whom I may have failed to contact again. This was due to the long timescale of putting everything together, by which time some chefs had moved to other establishments and I had lost others' contact details. I hope to be able to re-contact some of these chefs, and others, should there be the demand for a similar book in the future. I would also like to thank the students and staff at Cornwall College – St Austell for cooking, plating and photographing some of the recipes. My thanks also go to the Thistle Marble Arch, the Copthorne Tara, the Norfolk Royale and Holiday Inn hotels, whose complimentary accommodation allowed me to attend events at which I was able to meet both some of the contributing chefs and various supporters, thus raising further funds for my chosen charities that I did not anticipate prior to undertaking this project. Likewise, my thanks go to all those who agreed to support recipe pages. I am grateful to Action for Charity and Disability Cornwall, who helped with the sending out of questionnaires to Regainers and members of Disability Cornwall, and also to those members of the Spinal Injuries Association and Cornwall Blind Association who filled in questionnaires. Hopefully, by seeking feedback not exclusively from tetraplegics, a better understanding was reached of the needs and difficulties faced by other disabled people. I would also like to thank my PA/carers, friends, family and others who gave support and encouragement during this project, as at times things were not easy, especially when I was writing the introduction to the book. My thanks also go to Hospitality Action and Regain for their support, to those tetraplegics who agreed to be featured in the Dinner Party section and to everyone else who may have given support. My apologies if I have unintentionally missed anyone out. Though I devised the original layout in my own simple way, I would like to thank Sue Smith for putting the book together, along with John Such and Richard Elwell for their support with the covers. Finally, I would like to thank Ticky Donovan OBE, 9th Dan, for the Foreword and Brian Turner CBE for the Afterword. Last but not least, special thanks must go to Angus Clark of T.J. International, who agreed to the printing of a book some years ago and who, with this book, has honoured that earlier agreement.

List of Supporters

Active Assistance

1 Suffolk Way, Sevenoaks, TN13 1YL
Tel: 01732 779353
email: enquiries@activeassistance.com
web: www.activeassistance.com

Established in 1992, Active Assistance provides live-in care for adults & children with high level spinal cord injury and other physical disabilities, including progressive and neurological conditions.

The Active Hands Company

12 Rothwell Gardens, Woodley, Reading, Berkshire RG5 4TJ
Tel: +44 (0)118 9618481
email: info@activehands.co.uk
web: www.activehands.co.uk

Aids for those with limited hand function, enabling you to hold items firmly in your hand. Get a grip on activities you never thought possible, from DIY to skiing, from using gym equipment to cooking and playing on the Nintendo Wii.

Aubrey Allen

Unit 4, 3040 Siskin Parkway East, Middlemarch Business Park, Coventry CV3 4PE
Tel: 024 7642 2222
Fax: 024 7642 1555
email: sales@aubreyallen.co.uk
web: www.aubreyallen.co.uk

National Catering Butcher 2010, Aubrey Allen have grown their reputation on their uncompromising commitment to customer service and sourcing the very best of ethically reared British meat.

British Karate Federation (BKF)

58 Strathmore Avenue, Paisley, Scotland, PA1 3EE
Tel: +44 (0) 141 882 4880
email: info@britishkaratefederation.gb.com
web: www.britishkaratefederation.co.uk

The British Karate Federation is an umbrella body for the four Home Nations and represents Great Britain at world and Olympic levels.

Champagne Pol Roger

Shelton House, 4 Coningsby Street, Hereford, HR1 2DY
Tel: 01432 262 800
email: polroger@polroger.co.uk
web: www.polroger.co.uk

Pol Roger is a family company, one of the very last grandes marques remaining in the hands of the founding family. This independence of spirit and close family involvement in all stages of the business gives the champagnes their remarkable consistency.

Collins King & Associates

30 Maiden Lane, Covent Garden, London WC2E 7JS
Tel: 0207 240 0066
email: info@collinsking.co.uk
web: www.collinsking.co.uk

Established and independently owned hospitality recruitment consultancy whose primary focus is the sourcing of high calibre and experienced management, culinary and support personnel to the hospitality industry. Our extensive client base includes many of the UK's leading restaurants, hotel groups, contract catering and event companies.

Control Induction

Unit 2, Crowhurst Farm, Bullen Lane, East Peckham, Kent TN12 5LP
Tel: 01622 872821
email: info@controlinduction.co.uk
web: www.controlinduction.co.uk

Control Induction is a major supplier of bespoke and counter top induction hobs and French planchas. Our forte is producing custom made suites specifically to match client requirements.

Design Matters KBB Limited

Aries House, Straight Bit, Flackwell Heath, High Wycombe, Buckinghamshire, HP10 9NB
Tel: 01628 531584 Fax: 01628 532389
email: info@dmkbb.co.uk
web: www.dmkbb.co.uk
Home of the UK's finest accessible kitchens since 1997. We set the standards that others follow, with a truly unique design service and the expertise of Adam Thomas, the country's leading designer of accessible kitchens and an authority on accessible design.

Doble Quality Foods
Newdowns, St. Agnes, Cornwall TR5 0ST
Tel: 01872 552121
email: info@doblefoods.co.uk
web: www.doblefoods.co.uk

Doble Quality Foods have been supplying the catering trade in Cornwall for over sixty years. They are a Cornish owned family business committed to providing quality products and service. They are an established wholesaler of frozen, chilled and ambient goods.

Elior UK
Elior UK, Viewpoint, 240 London Road, Staines, TW18 4JT
Tel: 0845 20 35467
email: info@elior.co.uk
web: www.elior.co.uk

Elior UK is the market-leading catering, hospitality and facilities management group. We are passionate about providing great food, excellent customer service and exceptional value to all our clients.

Elliott Marketing & PR
Spring Cottage, 28 Spring Lane, Great Horwood, MK17 0QW
Tel: 01296 714745
email: ann@elliottmarketingpr.com
web: www.elliottmarketingpr.com

The UK's leading leisure, tourism and hospitality marketing and PR agency.

Hutton Hire
The Old Store, Trevemper, Newquay, Cornwall TR8 4QD
Tel: 01637 851801
email: enquiries@huttonhire.co.uk
web: www.huttonhire.co.uk

Hutton Hire is a local tool and small plant hire company based in Newquay Cornwall, it has been owned and run by Pete and Gail Hutton for over 20 years.

IndiCater Limited

Northfield House, Northfield End, Henley on Thames, Oxfordshire, RG9 2JG
Tel: 0333 240 0470
email: solutions@indicater.com
web: www.indicater.com

IndiCater provides web based back office management software across the hospitality industry. From Profit Management, Stock/Recipe Management, Employment/HR, Hospitality Ordering through to eProcurement, IndiCater helps reduce costs, increase sales, and improve margins.

Kavis Ltd

Unit 14, Pop-In Business Centre, South Way, Wembley, Middlesex HA9 0HF
Tel: 0844 8080 123
email: info@kavis.com
web: www.kavis.com

Provider of Food Preparation, Food Presentation, and Food Packaging solutions.

MacAce.net

Westcountry House, Victoria Square, Bodmin, Cornwall PL31 1EB
Tel: 01208 220010
email: info@macace.net
web: www.macace.net

Award winning hosting, email, broadband and Internet services specifically for Mac users.

Origin

7.0.6. Cameron House, White Cross, Lancaster LA1 4XQ
Tel: 01524 34100
email: info@origincare.com
web: www.origincare.com

Origin is an experienced specialist care agency providing long term or respite, 24 hour live-in care services for people with spinal cord injuries.

Premier Foods

Premier Foods, Premier House, Centrium Business Park,
Griffiths Way, St Albans,
Hertfordshire AL1 2RE
Tel: 01727 815850
email: marketing@premierfoods.co.uk
web: www.premierfoods.co.uk

Premier Foods is the UK's largest food producer; a great British food company with a passion for creating great food and brands that people love. The foodservice division exists to supply the needs of all cooks, chefs and caterers throughout the industry through our wide range of products including Bisto, Sharwoods, McDougalls and 39 other brands.

Professional Fitness & Education

9a Cleasby Road, Menston, Ilkley, LS29 6JE
Tel: 01943 879816
email: info@pfetraining.co.uk
web: www.pfetraining.co.uks

Award winning organisation providing private educational courses in teaching NVQ level 2/3/4 in fitness training, personal training, special populations, Pilates and Yoga.

Rational UK Ltd

Unit 4, Titan Court, Laporte Way, Luton, Beds LU4 8EF
Tel: 01582 480388
email: andy.bridgeman@rational-uk.co.uk
web: www.rational-online.com/GB_en

Rational are the world's leading manufacturers of combination ovens. The Rational Self Cooking Center provides state-of-the-art technology that is simple to use and provides perfect results every time – at the touch of a button.

Restaurant Magazine

William Reed Business Media
Broadfield Park, Crawley, West Sussex RH11 9RT
Tel: 01293 613400
email: editorial@restaurantmagazine.co.uk
web: www.bighospitality.co.uk

Restaurant magazine is the leading title for the restaurant industry with a circulation of over 16,000 individuals in the UK, primarily made up of chefs and restaurateurs. It also produces the globally renowned S. Pellegrino World's 50 Best Restaurants Awards, as well as the UK's National Restaurant Awards.

Rhug Organic

Rhug Estate Office, Corwen, Denbighshire LL21 0EH
Tel: 01490 413000
email: lordnewborough@rhug.co.uk
web: www.rhug.co.uk

Meat Wholesalers/ Straight Retailers.

Spinal Homecare Ltd

157 Stricklandgate, Kendal, Cumbria LA9 4RF
Tel: 01539 730777
email: karen.mason@spinalhomecare.co.uk
web: www.spinalhomecare.co.uk

Specialist providers of high quality live-in care throughout the UK to people with a Spinal Cord Injury or other similar disability.

St Austell Brewery Co Ltd

63 Trevarthian Road, St Austell, Cornwall, PL25 4BY
Tel: 0845 241 1122
email: info@staustellbrewery.co.uk
web: www.staustellbrewery.co.uk

Founded in 1851 by Walter Hicks, St Austell Brewery is a family run business that has been brewing award-winning superb ales ever since and has over 170 pubs in Cornwall, Devon and Somerset where you can be sure to enjoy a friendly welcome, plus great food and beer.

Tante Marie School of Cookery

Tante Marie Ltd, Woodham House, Carlton Road, Woking, Surrey GU21 4HF
Tel: 01483 726957
email: info@tantemarie.co.uk
web: www.tantemarie.co.uk

Tante Marie, the UK's oldest independent cookery school, was bought by Gordon Ramsay, together with the school's principal, Andrew Maxwell, in 2008. The school offers a range of courses, from 1 and 2 days up to a full professional diploma, lasting 1 year.

3663

3663 Business Support Centre, Buckingham Court,
Kingsmead Business Park, London Road, High Wycombe
HP11 1JU
Tel: 0370 3663 100
email: 3663corporate@3663.co.uk

3663 is one of the UK's leading foodservice companies, providing
complete catering solutions to customers of all sizes and
capabilities, within the foodservice market.

Tibard Ltd

Tibard House, Broadway, Dukinfield, Cheshire SK16 4UU
Tel: 0161 342 1000
email: sales@tibard.co.uk
web: www.tibard.co.uk

Tibard offer a fully managed uniform service, ranging from the direct
purchase of garments to chefs' wear rental and laundry services on
a nationwide scale. Tibard's ethos is flexibility; we are able to design
and manufacture bespoke garments or offer off the peg items at
competitive prices.

Unilever Food Solutions

Unilever House, Springfield Drive, Leatherhead,
Surrey KT22 7GR
Tel: 01372 9450000
email: ray.lorimer@unilever.com
web: www.knorr.co.uk

Food manufacturer of major foodservice brands such as KNORR,
HELLMANNS, COLMANS and PG Tips.

Vigilance Resources Ltd

7b High Street, Fenstanton, Cambridgeshire, PE28 9LQ
Tel: +44 (0)) 1480 832424
Mob: +44 (0) 7767 761 858
email: vigilanceresourcesltd2010@hotmail.co.uk

Specialists in supplying Close Protection worldwide, teaching
/lecturing on Close Protection to SIA (Security Industry Authority)
standards, and supplying Residence Security Teams to high profile
clients. Mike Billman, Managing Director, has been in Close
Protection since 1980.

Winckworth Sherwood
Minerva House, 5 Montague Close, London, SE1 9BB
Tel: 020 7593 5000
email: info@wslaw.co.uk
web: www.wslaw.co.uk

Winckworth Sherwood solicitors provide a range of legal services to the leisure and hospitality industry. We advise on all areas of the law; buying and selling businesses, applying for alcohol licences, employment law and commercial contracts.

Over three years ago David contacted me, among many others, about his proposed book. As with most busy chefs, I eventually got round to helping him!

Anyone involved with this project has come to recognise that David has tremendous courage and a determination that puts many of us to shame. As a doer, a tireless go-getter and a lover of great food he has my total admiration, and I can only say well done, chef, you set out to do it and you did it!

So what's this book about? Well, David's aim is to make eating out or at home easier for disabled people, as well as to support the industry charity Hospitality Action and Regain – The Trust for Sports Tetraplegics. While he has always had a clear vision of what he wanted to achieve with this book, David is aware that some of the recipes may not meet the desired criteria and has covered these areas in his introduction and elsewhere. As such I hope chefs in Britain and around the world are willing to take on board some of his and others' suggestions as to how to make food easier to eat.

Our industry focuses on people and demonstrates how important each individual is to creating and maintaining standards. Hence, the more individual needs are catered for within our industry and the more inclusive it aims to be, the better. When David first made contact I was surprised at how similar his early career was to my own. I also spent time working for the Savoy Group and at the Savoy Grill and also worked in Bermuda. I am therefore very aware of the sort of life he would have been leading prior to his accident and how devastating it must have been. However, in the face of adversity he has achieved good things for our industry and in many other areas over the years.

We initially met when he attended the Bournemouth Hotel & Catering Show drumming up further support for his charities, and we would also meet at the after-show dinner in aid of Hospitality Action. This is where David's humour came to the fore. Much to everyone's amusement, he won the main prize that evening while competing against four ladies in ballgowns. As the prize was unsuitable for a wheelchair user he graciously handed it to one of the ladies.

Having read in these pages how others have been injured similarly to David, I feel fortunate indeed that my own career has been injury free. While it cannot have been easy to compile, I feel that David has achieved an admirable combination of life story and cookbook – one that will make an inspiring read for those in the hospitality industry and elsewhere.

Good luck, David.

Brian Turner CBE

Simon Haigh
Mallory Court Hotel
Harbury Lane, Leamington Spa,
Warwickshire CV33 9QB
Tel: 01926 330214
www.mallory.co.uk

Gary Rhodes
www.garyrhodes.com

Nathan Outlaw
Nathan Outlaw Restaurants Ltd
St Enodoc Hotel, Rock,
Cornwall PL27 6LA
Tel: 01208 863394
www.nathan-outlaw.com

Lars Windfuhr
Hyatt Regency London – The Churchill
30 Portman Square, London W1H 7BH
Tel: 020 7486 5800
www.london.churchill.hyatt.com

Simon Gueller
Boxtree Restaurant
35-37 Church Street, Ilkley,
West Yorkshire LS29 9DR
Tel: 01943 608484
www.theboxtree.co.uk

Tom Aikens
Tom Aikens Restaurant
3 Elystan Street, Chelsea,
London, SW3 3NT
Tel: 020 7584 2003
www.tomaikens.co.uk

Brett Camborne-Paynter
Austells

10 Beach Road, Carlyon Bay,
St Austell, Cornwall
Tel: 01726 813 888
www.austells.net

Cyrus Todiwala
Café Spice Namasté
16 Prescot Street, London E1 8AZ
Tel: 020 7488 9242
www.cafespice.co.uk

Mike Monahan
www.pocruises.com

Marco Pierre White
www.marcopierrewhite.org

Peter Gordon
The Providores and Tapa Room
109 Marylebone High Street,
London W1U 4RX
Tel: 020 7935 6175
www.peter-gordon.net

Mark Hix
Hix Oyster & Chop House
36-37 Greenhill Rents, Cowcross Street
London EC1M 6BN
Tel: 020 7017 1930
www.restaurantsetcltd.co.uk

Galton Blackiston
Morston Hall
Morston, Holt, Norfolk NR25 7AA
Tel: 01263 741041
www.morstonhall.com

Michael Kitts
The Emirates Academy of Hospitality

Management
PO Box 29662, Umm Suqeim 3,
str. 10c, bld. 69, opp Burj al Arab,
Dubai, United Arab Emirates
Tel: +971 4 315 5555
info@emiratesacademy.edu

Martin Burge
Whatley Manor
Easton Grey, Malmesbury, Wiltshire
SN16 0RB
Tel: 01666 822 888
www.whatleymanor.com

John Williams
The Ritz
150 Piccadilly, London W1J 9BR
Tel: 020 7493 8181
www.theritzlondon.com

Adam Byatt
Trinity
4 The Polygon, Clapham,
London SW4 0JG
Tel: 020 7622 1199
www.trinityrestaurant.co.uk

Kevin Viner
Viners Restaurant
Carvynick Farm, Summercourt,
Newquay TR8 5AF
Tel: 01872 510544
www.vinersrestaurant.co.uk

Chris Galvin
www.galvinrestaurants.com

Gordon Ramsay
www.gordonramsay.com

Gareth Billington
Everton Football Club
Goodison Park, Liverpool L4 4EL
Tel: 0871 663 1878
www.evertonfc.com

Mark Askew
www.gordonramsay.com

Mitch Tonks
The Rockfish Grill
128 Whiteladies Road, Clfiton, Bristol
BS8 2RS
Tel: 01179 737384
www.mitchtonks.co.uk

Grant Mather
Cornwall College – St Austell
Tregonissey Road, St Austell PL25 4DJ
Tel: 01726 226626
www.cornwall.ac.uk

Paul Ainsworth
Number 6 Restaurant
6 Middle Street, Padstow, Cornwall
PL28 8AP
Tel: 01841 532 093
www.number6inpadstow.co.uk

James Tanner
Tanners Restaurant
Prysten House, Finewell Street,
Plymouth PL1 2AE
Tel: 01752 252001
www.tannersrestaurant.com

Edmund Smith
Ascot's Restaurant at the Royal Palms
24 Rosemont Avenue, Hamilton,

Bermuda
www.ascots.bm

Clyde Hollett
Bournemouth Highcliff Marriott Hotel
St. Michael's Road, West Cliff,
Bournemouth BH2 5DU
www.marriott.co.uk

James Martin
www.jamesmartinchef.co.uk

Simon Hulstone
The Elephant Restaurant

3 & 4 Beacon Terrace, Torquay,
Devon TQ1 2BH
Tel: 01803 200 044
www.elephantrestaurant.co.uk

Gino D'Acampo
www.ginodacampo.com

Ruth Hinks
Chocolate & Pastry School
Unit 7, Southpark Industrial Estate
Peebles EH45 9ED
Tel: 01721 723 764
www.cocoablack.co.uk

Some cooking terms explained

al dente – literally, 'to the tooth'; retaining a slight resistance in the centre after cooking

bain-marie – a double boiler in which foods can be gently cooked away from the heat source

broiler – a pan for oven cooking with a slotted rack and a base for catching the drips

brown butter – butter cooked until it browns

butter monté – an emulsified sauce made by whisking butter together with a little water

coulis – a thick sauce made with puréed fruit or vegetables

crème anglaise – a light pouring custard made with sugar, egg yolks and hot milk and flavoured with vanilla

to deglaze – to use a liquid to remove cooked-on residue from a pan and reduce to a sauce or gravy

duxelle – a finely chopped mixture of mushrooms, shallots and herbs

to emulsify – to combine together by whisking two liquids which normally do not mix easily, such as oil and vinegar when making a mayonnaise

to flambé – to pour brandy or other liqueur over food and ignite it

ganache – a mixture of melted chocolate and cream

to julienne – to cut into long, thin strips like matchsticks

jus lié – meat juices thickened with cornflour or arrowroot

kadhai – a deep, circular metal cooking pot used in Indian cooking

quenelle – a small portion of soft food shaped into an oval

to sauté – to fry quickly over a high heat

tempered chocolate – chocolate which has been precisely heated to give it a glossy appearance

velouté – a light stock-based white sauce